DOUG BIEGEL

The Baker's Son

I met Doug the summer of 1994, and over the past twenty-seven years God has used his friendship and phone calls to encourage me and to remind me that God always has a plan. Reading Doug's story took me on a roller-coaster ride of smiles and tears. Mostly, Doug's story reminded me of God's faithfulness and challenged me not to be afraid of pointing people to God's love in Jesus Christ.

Whether you are young or old, if you are in need of inspiration, encouragement and motivation, pick up this book and enjoy a terrific read. It may be just the medicine from God your heart needs.

Pastor Mike Pitsenberger
Overisel Reformed Church
Holland, Michigan

The Baker's Son

Copyright © 2021 by Doug Biegel. All rights reserved.

Cover design by Barry Smith. Interior design by Dean H. Renninger.

All Scripture quotations, unless otherwise indicated, are taken from the Holy Bible, *New International Version*,® *NIV*.® Copyright © 1973, 1978, 1984, 2011 by Biblica, Inc.® Used by permission. All rights reserved worldwide.

Jeremiah 29:11 in chapter 8 and Jeremiah 29:12-14 in chapter 9 are taken from *THE MESSAGE*, copyright © 1993, 1994, 1995, 1996, 2000, 2001, 2002 by Eugene H. Peterson. Used by permission of NavPress. All rights reserved. Represented by Tyndale House Publishers.

Proverbs 3:5-6 in chapters 11 and 12 is taken from the Holy Bible, Modern English Version. Copyright © 2014 by Military Bible Association. Published and distributed by Charisma House.

Lamentations 3:22-23 in chapter 12 is taken from *The Holy Bible*, English Standard Version® (ESV®), copyright © 2001 by Crossway, a publishing ministry of Good News Publishers. Used by permission. All rights reserved.

Published in the United States by Lucas Lane Publishers.

26 25 24 23 22 21 20
7   6   5   4   3   2   1

"For I know the plans I have for you," declares the Lord, "plans to prosper you and not to harm you, plans to give you hope and a future."

—JEREMIAH 29:11—

Life is uncertain. Eat dessert first.

—ERNESTINE ULMER—

TEAM BIEGEL

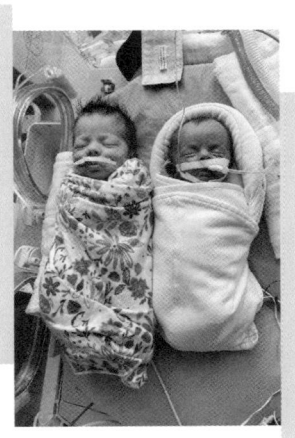

DEDICATION

I want to dedicate this book to my Lord and Savior, Jesus Christ, who gave His life so that I can have life with Him. His grace is too amazing for me to get my arms around.

I want to dedicate this book to my wife Debbie, whose love for me has been indescribable and who ran an amazing home. She was the captain of our home and she kept order in our house. I have been able to serve the Lord on the school board and church board and in parent-church activities knowing that everything is good at home. Home is top for me. Without her love I couldn't have done this.

I want to dedicate this book to my children—Pam and Dan, Amy and Al, Mark and Marissa, Jana and Brent, Paul and Kayla—and my ten grandchildren—Trevor, Ashlee, Drew, Ethan, Isaac, Tyler, Zeke, Nina, Mollee, and Megan. I want them to know that walking with Jesus is the most important thing.

My life is complete because of my family. My greatest source of joy comes from them. This is my love letter to all of you.

This is one man's journey and one man's walk of God's faithfulness in good times and bad. While you read this, be thinking of your story. God wants us to be able to share the story He has given each of us with others. Always be prepared; you never know who can relate to your story unless you are willing to share your story with them.

INTRODUCTION

God's Amazing Grace and My Big Mouth

Everybody has a story, but we often don't have the time or opportunity to share it.

I started openly telling mine in 2002 when I began working as a salesman for a large pharmaceutical company. In Sales 101, we learn that you have to be able to sell your product in the time it takes for an elevator ride. However, my story didn't involve anything I was selling. I simply wanted to share what Jesus had done in my life.

There was a part of me that changed in my late forties. I developed what I call a "holy boldness." People couldn't fire me for sharing my story. So whenever I got the chance, I would give my elevator speech.

"Let me share what happened in my life. In ten months' time, I bought a home, had a child, had major surgery, and then witnessed a fire to my family business that wiped out everything. Seven and a half years later, I woke up and my wife, Marilyn, was dead in bed."

Needless to say, this usually led to a few more questions from the person I was talking to. People wanted to know what happened and how I got through everything. This opened many opportunities to witness for Jesus Christ. My biggest joy in life is having an opportunity to share my story and how God has impacted me.

My MO has never been to hit people over the head with the Bible, and that's not my intention when I open up to others. I'm not there to say, "This is what Jesus Christ said." I'm there to walk a mile in your shoes, good or bad. And to come alongside you. I have to earn the right to share Jesus Christ with you, and I can't do that until I know you and walk with you for a while. Until I know what brings you joy and what hurts inside you. One way I can walk a mile with someone is to tell them my story.

Whoever you might be, please consider this book as my chance to walk a mile with you. Since I'm the only person talking here, I get to share my story with you. I've believed for a long time that each of us has a story, but so many of us are afraid to communicate it.

As the title of this chapter says, I'm here because of God's amazing grace and my big mouth.

This is one man's journey from baking to steel. More importantly, it's the story of God's faithfulness in good times and bad.

CHAPTER ONE

My Parents

There are three main ingredients that go into the almond filling I use to make my banket: almond paste, sugar, and eggs (along with a lot of love!). My whole upbringing always included three key ingredients as well. These were faith, family, and church. Since I was a child, if something didn't include one of those three things, our family probably didn't do it.

I had a fairly normal childhood, unless you think living above a bakery is not normal. It took many years before I realized the impact the bakery has had on my life. As the eldest child of Joseph and Greta Biegel, one of the many blessings I had was being able to see my parents every day.

Every day I saw firsthand how hard my dad worked. Each morning on my way to school, I said hi to him, and many days he ended up bringing me. After school, I would see him still toiling away in his shop. I spent most of my young life in the apartment above my parents' bakery. Whenever I thought about my future and what I would do when I grew up, I don't think I ever thought beyond the bakery. I was destined to be a baker, just like my father and grandfather.

When I was a young child, I'd crack the eggs for my grandfather and father. Every two and a half dozen eggs I cracked, I would be rewarded with a banana. Ironic how I'd be given something healthy when I was helping them create some sweet pastry or cake. I grew up learning the craft and always asking myself how I could become a better baker.

I loved my father and wanted to be with him as much as I could. He was my best friend on earth and I enjoyed spending time with him.

My father learned to bake from his father, Joseph Sr.

MY PARENTS

Right before the Great Depression, my grandfather bought the bakery we lived above and moved his family from Spring Lake, Michigan. Joseph Sr. had been taught to bake from the Braak's Bakery. Joseph and Carrie lived in an apartment above Biegel's Bakery while he worked hard to build it up.

After my father, Joseph Jr., graduated from high school, he opened up a bunch of storefront bakeries around the area. When my dad went to war, my grandfather closed the Biegel's Bakery stores one by one. By the time my father came back from the war, he was told by my grandfather that the bakery was his.

There were two apartments above the bakery. You had to walk up a flight of stairs to get to them. They were beautiful. My grandparents lived in one side and we lived in the other. This meant I had the opportunity to see my grandparents every day. Dad bought one newspaper and I would have to run sections of it between both apartments. I lived my whole life above the bakery, which meant I didn't have a backyard with grass in it until the fall of 1971 when we moved to South Holland.

There are many things I inherited and learned from my father. One of those is my work ethic. Another is my self-confidence, which is interesting since my father was normally quiet. Dad never said no to me. "You can do that," he would always tell me. "You can do that." He let me try to do whatever thing I set my mind to do, including building a minibike that he wanted nothing to do with.

It's amazing what encouragement can do to an individual.

Of course he was a disciplinarian, but I had a tremendous amount of respect for him since I saw how hard he worked for our family. From the time he woke up to the time he went to bed, he was always working. I'm sure he started at four or five in the morning and went to six or seven every night. He never asked anybody to do anything he would not do. Joseph Biegel led by example.

My dad was my best friend on earth, bar none. What a blessing.

In many ways, my father is one of the reasons I'm writing this book. My dad has been gone since July 2004. I'd like to know more stories, to ask him about his youth and upbringing, to understand what sorts of things helped shape and form the man he became. I know some of the tales, but they go through my filter.

MY PARENTS

When I think of my children and grandchildren, I want them to be able to retell my story to others.

My mother is the youngest child of Peter and Sadie Tuinstra. Growing up in Roseland, on the far south side of Chicago, Greta Doris Tuinstra attended Roseland Christian School and Pullman Tech for high school. As a teenager, she began working at Biegel's Bakery with some of her high school friends. Soon she began dating my father and October 22, 1949, they were married. Her parents and family attended church, and as a young girl, she began her love for the Lord that continues to this day.

These are the most important things Joseph and Greta Biegel taught me. At a young age, my parents modeled loving the Lord with all their heart, soul, mind, and strength. They showed me how to be generous with my time, my talents, and my money, and they demonstrated how these traits could impact other people. This was my foundation.

In sharing my story, I'd like to be able to leave something for my children and grandchildren so they can know the foundation I was built on. I want them to know that I love Jesus Christ and I'm amazed by His grace. I want to show them and anybody else I can the different seasons of my life. The sunrises and the storms and the sunsets. I want to leave footprints in the sand that will lead them to the Cross. That's all I care about. That's all my parents cared about, too.

CHAPTER TWO

The Decision

"The bus will wait."

These four words changed my life.

In the summer of 1962, I was part of history when I attended a Billy Graham crusade with my church. From May 30 to June 17 of that year, the famed and beloved preacher came to Chicago for his Greater Chicago Crusade. For nineteen days, Graham preached the gospel to forty thousand people at McCormick Place and to a hundred thousand people at Soldier Field. Over seven hundred thousand men, women, and children attended this crusade, and there were sixteen thousand commitments made to Christ.

Thank God I was one of them.

I was nine years old at the time, and God was working in my heart. Like so many people, I was moved by Billy Graham's simple message.

"Who is Jesus?" the evangelist asked the crowd.

I had grown up in a Christian family, watching the example of my parents. I attended Roseland Christian School. I was blessed to have many impactful youth sponsors while growing up. By now I was old enough to be thinking of these things, to be wondering what a relationship with Jesus Christ truly meant.

"Yes, He was a teenager," Graham reminded us. "He went through some of the growing-up processes that you're going through. He's been there!"

This evangelist was now revealing what this Jesus my parents followed was all about.

"We recognize He was a great man," Billy Graham stated. "But we don't want that cross where He died for sin. We want everything but that. But I want to tell you this—you can never enter the Kingdom of God unless you come to the cross. And you can never enter the Kingdom of God unless you're willing to identify yourself with Christ at the cross. Because Jesus hung openly and unashamedly for you on that cross. He died for you. And you must come and be willing to die with Him. You must be willing to go back to that day."

Of course by now I knew what came next. Jesus didn't stay on that cross or in that tomb. On the third day He rose again. The evangelist brilliantly proclaimed what happened next.

"It was the resurrection of Christ that caused the disciples to go out and turn the world upside down. They went everywhere saying, 'Christ is alive!'"

By the end of this stirring sermon, my soul was being shaken. I was presented with a very real dilemma inside my heart as Graham continued to talk.

"Whether you like it or not, you're going to make a decision today. You say, 'Oh no I'm not.' Yes, you are. You're going to make a decision today. Some of you are going to ridicule Him. You're going to ridicule what I say. You'll ridicule Christ. Then, some of you won't reject Him. You'll just neglect Him. You won't make a decision one way or another. You can neglect Christ long enough until you reject Him."

THE BAKER'S SON

I didn't want to ridicule or reject this person who died for me. I didn't want to neglect this decision.

"There are others today that are going to receive Him. 'Yes, I'm going to make this decision.' You've got to decide about Him. And when you decide, you decide by your will."

It felt like Billy Graham was only speaking to me. When he urged people to come forward and make that step of faith, I couldn't help worrying about the ride back home with my young people's group from church. What if they left without me?

"The bus will wait," Graham announced. "Don't worry about the bus."

So I got out of my seat and made that decision. I accepted that Jesus was more than a man, that He was indeed God. As Graham said, "Jesus was His name but Christ was His title." I asked for forgiveness of my sins and gave my life to God.

The bus did indeed wait for me. Soon after this, I made my public profession of faith in my church. He has been my Savior and Lord ever since. God has been so faithful to me, even when I have disappointed Him.

Now all these years later, whenever I'm talking to someone about faith issues, I can tell them, "Don't you worry about the bus. I'll take you home."

CHAPTER THREE

Shady Shores

Some of the worst things in life can produce the greatest blessings you'll ever have. This happened in my life when I was fourteen years old.

On Father's Day weekend in 1967, my family and I were visiting my grandfather at a hospital in Holland, Michigan. He had gotten sick and was suffering from cancer. While we were there, we decided to visit a place we had heard about called Shady Shores. Since we knew some of the families who had houses around the lake, they had told us about the chapel and the trailer park across from it. So that weekend, we decided to check out the park called Shady Shores.

Mom always thought we were missing a yard as children since we lived in an apartment above the bakery. She never really liked it, not the way she would have enjoyed a house with a big lawn and a garden in the back. I'll be honest: we never wanted for anything as kids. We had a pool and a swing set on the roof, and our apartment contained six rooms, so we had plenty. This didn't change our mother's mind, however; she always felt like we were missing out not having grass underneath our feet the moment we stepped out of our front door.

That Father's Day weekend, after riding by Gun Lake Chapel, we walked to the trailer park right across the street to look for a possible place to rent. The rows of trailers were in the same spots as they are today, but the lanes weren't paved yet. The owner of Shady Shores told us he had one place that would fit our family and another that wouldn't. So he showed us the first one, a trailer on Fir Lane that was forty-five feet from the lake. We were all blown away.

Oh, my stars, I thought. *This is utopia!*

At the time, there were around a hundred families in Shady Shores. Few of the residents made improvements on their trailers since the owner of the park could sometimes be difficult to deal with. It was only when all the families bought the park that improvements on the trailers began to be made.

My parents decided on purchasing this trailer, and thus a new life began. I couldn't believe the trailer was ours. As soon as it turned warm, my schedule remained the same. On Saturdays, I worked from four in the morning until 3 p.m., then would climb into a car and drive to Gun Lake. I'd swim and ski until I couldn't stand or see, then would go to bed and pass out. On Sunday mornings, we always went to church as a family. We were happy to attend Sunday school at Gun Lake Chapel; then we would come back and get into the lake as soon as possible. Back then, we were among the few kids who could actually go into the water on Sundays. We would have a fast lunch and then dive in, and we would remain in the lake until church later that evening. Then after a light supper, I'd drive back to Illinois in order to be at work Monday morning. My father and mother would stay behind at the lake.

I'd run the bakery on Mondays and Tuesdays while

THE BAKER'S SON

Dad stayed at the lake. On Tuesday afternoon, I'd drive up to Gun Lake with a friend. Like a relay racer tagging a teammate, Dad would head home to run the bakery while I stayed and spent Wednesday at the lake. We would ski all day and Mom would feed us. We would drive back home, work our butts off Thursday, Friday, and Saturday, then repeat it all over again.

This wasn't just a season of our lives. This *became* our lives. It's still today a big part of our lives.

I can picture Dad selling bakery goods up and down the lanes of Shady Shores. There were lots of children for my sisters and me to play with at the lake. Spending summers at the lake became a big deal for our whole family. To this day, my mom and my sister Janice have the same trailer that we had when I was a kid. My married sister Joy and her husband, Gary, have a unit, and my wife Debbie and I have one too. Gun Lake is our oasis, our happy place. We just finished our fifty-fourth summer there.

My grandfather's passing in 1971 after we purchased the trailer at Gun Lake became a watermark on my life. So did that trailer and lake. God can always bring light out of the darkness. You simply have to believe He can.

CHAPTER FOUR

Growing Up

Faith, family, and school. These were the three legs of the tripod that kept our family together. Chances are if it didn't involve one of these three things, we didn't participate in it. My sisters and I could see how important these were to our parents, so they became a vital part of our lives, too.

First off, it was clear that Jesus Christ was very important to my parents. Dad was an elder and deacon at First Reformed Church of Roseland, and he served

THE BAKER'S SON

with his father on the mission board. My father had a heart for the less fortunate. Once a month, he would go down to Westside Rescue Mission bringing all the items in the bakery that didn't sell to give to people on the street. We always had a special-needs person around the bakery, doing odd jobs like washing pots and pans.

My mom was a godly lady and still is! To this day she keeps a prayer journal. My mother is a prayer warrior who prays for very specific things. I'll constantly be giving her descriptive prayer requests. "Mom, I have a job coming up and I need seven welders." She'll write that down in her journal and pray for exactly that.

My parents encouraged us to be involved in church activities. I was very active in Sunday school and our youth group. My parents always sent us to summer camps, and I was fortunate to see other people model and live out their faith in Jesus Christ apart from Mom and Dad. I went to HoneyRock Camp in Wisconsin and a YMCA camp called Camp Pinewood, as well as Camp Manitoqua.

It was a blessing to have two parents who loved each other. They modeled that well. The family was such a huge priority to my parents. I remember going over to my uncle Bill and aunt Alice's house on Sundays for dinner. Every time we went, we always brought an uncooked pot roast, and as a kid I never could understand why since my aunt would already have a pot roast ready for our meal. I finally realized my aunt would freeze the pot roast for the next time we came over since they couldn't afford it.

My father had two sisters: one was married with two children and the other wasn't married. Aunt Albertha was a missionary to India, so I grew accustomed to having a missionary in our house. Every time a doctor from India came to Chicago, they had to stop at our house. We learned to eat chicken and curry. Our home was always a very welcoming, safe, and comforting place. My parents entertained a lot, and we had lots of people staying with us as I was growing up.

On my mother's side, she had four brothers, meaning there were a plethora of cousins all around us for Thanksgiving, Christmas, and birthdays. Many of them went to our school. To this day, our cousins get together every so often for pizza.

I was a typical kid during my high school years at Chicago Christian. To be honest, I wasn't a very good student—I was lazy. I played basketball and football but was never a good athlete. As I say jokingly, the

Biegels are athletically challenged. Sports were never one of our gifts.

I had a tremendous respect for my father and how hard he worked, so I didn't stray much from the rules or deviate far from the norm. I didn't want to ruffle his feathers. I had some rebellious moments in junior high and early in high school, but I quickly learned how to straighten out. I remember once when I was fourteen or fifteen taking the car out without asking, then downshifting from third gear to reverse and blowing out the trans or the clutch. This was probably the worst thing I ever did as a teen. I remember hanging up the keys where they belonged, then being woken up by my father early in the morning since he couldn't use his car for deliveries.

I don't remember my punishment. Perhaps the worst was knowing I had let down my father. I didn't want to disappoint both my father and my heavenly Father.

I was the firstborn in our family; Joy and Janice arrived not long after me. I don't ever remember not getting along with my sisters. Both are teachers and very educated, with Joy being a professor at a Christian college while Janice has been teaching over twenty-five years at a Christian grade school. It's interesting how both of them went into education. Trust me—they're a lot smarter than I am. I was always the big brother interested in the bakery. All of us share a common commitment in loving and impacting people. That's our shared DNA.

During those foundational and impressionable years, my life revolved around my parents, our church, and school. My friends came from a combination of Christian Reformed and Reformed churches. Every year my family went away on vacation for two weeks, usually going to a lake in southwest Michigan. My grandfather would come and run the bakery while we were gone, and he did this until he was unable.

Growing up, I knew my destiny always lay in the bakery. *That's where I'm going* was the attitude I took. I don't think it was ever an option not to work. By the time I reached sixteen, I was involved with the bakery along with my sisters.

After graduating from high school, I went to a junior college, figuring this would be enough of an education to run the family business. I had a flexible schedule working for my father, but I didn't apply myself as I should have. It would be years later when I earned a degree in business management from Olivet Nazarene

University, but by then I already had learned more than enough in the world of business.

I worked for my father at the bakery from 1971 until 1978. The fire made us move on from the bakery, but I'm still baking to this day over forty years later.

CHAPTER FIVE

Starting a Life Together

She always had a smile on her face. That's one of the things I remember most about Marilyn.

Like so many sweet things in my life, baking brought us together. While I delivered bread every day to the Holland Home, I began to notice a pretty girl who worked there. Marilyn Venhuizen was a bubbly and outgoing girl who was still in high school at the time. She was one of the servers at Holland Home who worked a different station every day. One day, a server might be working on setting the salt, pepper, and sugar out on tables, while another was responsible for utensils. There was a station dedicated to the bread. It didn't take me long to realize Marilyn was working at the bread station every day just to see me.

I had already graduated high school, so it took me a while to ask her out. Marilyn had lost her father early in life, and she and her family struggled. Yet there was a joy that radiated out of Marilyn, and this came from her love of Jesus Christ. She would always be smiling in spite of how things might be. Her three pillars in life mirrored mine: faith, family, and church. She was a believer and came from a great home with a wonderful family.

By the time Marilyn graduated high school in June of '74, we were both in love. For her graduation present, I ordered a hope chest for her, but they said it wouldn't be delivered for six to eight weeks, so I ended up also buying her a ten-speed bike. It just so happened the hope chest came in on the day she graduated, so Marilyn received both the chest and the bike. Not long after this, I asked her mother if I could marry her. We married in July 1975.

Life was good. I'd married this amazing and wonderful girl. Almost two years later on June 15, 1977, Pam was welcomed into our family. Our little family was started. We bought our first house the same year.

God was good.

I was working hard in the bakery while we started to raise a family. Marilyn loved being home with the children. She wasn't high-maintenance in any way; if her family was good, then Marilyn was happy. She loved her family.

We were a growing, young couple. Loving life. Having a great time.

In January of '78, I would have a major surgery. Then ten weeks after that, the bakery would be ravaged by fire. Everything my parents had worked so hard to build and every part of the business we owned and operated burned to the ground.

The bakery started in the late twenties, and my father took it over from his dad in 1945 after World War II. For fifty years, our family business had provided treats for customers. It only took seven hours to completely destroy the bakery.

But God was faithful.

That's been the theme of my life. God's faithfulness

in good times and bad. One of those really bad moments had arrived. I look back now and see God's fingerprints over those times.

CHAPTER SIX

The Fire

"There's smoke coming from the front of the bakery."

It was March 31, 1978, and I knew this phone call wasn't an April Fools' joke. The clerk from the bakery sounded stressed on the other end of the line. I told her I'd be there shortly. My parents were at a wedding, so I couldn't reach them.

I took the highway to get to the bakery. After getting off the exit, I could see the whole western sky filled with flames. I knew this was bad. Half of the Chicago Fire

Department was there trying to put out this three-alarm fire on a Friday night.

The fire was devastating. It rocked my world and challenged everything I knew. Everything my father and I owned was gone. I didn't know what he was going to do for work, nor did I have any idea what I'd be doing, either. I was twenty-five years old, with a wife and daughter and mortgage, and I didn't know where my next paycheck would come from.

After spending the following day reeling and looking over the destruction, our whole family was in church on Sunday morning. Back in the day, the leaders of the church would get together before the service and pray, and this morning was no different. My father was an elder and I was a deacon, so we were both there. I always made it a habit to shake everybody's hands when we first got together. The last person I walked up to was my father, and by the time I got to him, I was weeping. I put my arms around my father and tried to encourage him.

"It's going to be all right," I whispered.

The truth was I didn't know if things would be all right. I had faith, but I also had fears. A lot of fears.

That night at church, a spinster lady and her sister

came up to me. My father had befriended them like so many people.

"Dougie, your father and your family have been such a blessing to us."

Before I knew it, she began to peel off twenty-dollar bills, one right after another, putting them in my hand.

"Half of these are for you, and half are for your father."

I didn't know how to accept this gift. I'd never had to take anything like this in my life.

Later that evening, an elder from our church asked to speak with me in private. I didn't have much of a relationship with him. I just knew he arrived in America straight off the boat from the old country in Holland.

"Doug, I want to make your house payment. I don't want you ever to tell anybody."

This man assured me that he didn't care how long it would take for me to get back on my feet. He would make my house payment.

I can admit this was difficult to accept. Yes, I'm Dutch and I'm proud. I don't want to be on the receiving end; I want to be on the giving end. I learned by example. The people in our church were generous, and our church family rallied around us.

Years later, when this man's son John got married, I shared this story with him and his future bride Laurel. I told them the cake I brought to the wedding was their gift in honor of what their father had done for me. Then, in March of 2018, when John and Laurel's daughter, Annie, got married, I did the same thing. I told her the story of my bakery burning down.

"This cake is a gift from Debbie and me because of what your grandfather did in 1978," I said. "You need to pay it forward at some point."

To this day, I am still very good friends with John and Laurel.

The past year had proven to be the very embodiment of God's faithfulness in good times and bad. There had been so much to celebrate: purchasing our first house in April of '77 and welcoming Pam two months later. But there had been tough times even before the fire. Ten weeks before seeing the bakery burn to the ground, doctors removed four feet of my intestines in a surgery. I had just started getting back on my feet when the fire happened.

The surgery was a result of a drinking problem. I

hid my addiction from those closest to me. Thankfully, I was only addicted to cola and not liquor, but still I was drinking an eight-pack of cola every day. Before getting to work at five or six each morning, I'd consume two sodas, then would have more throughout the day. My father was busy running a bakery, so he didn't know about the two sodas I had before and after work. Marilyn never saw the colas I drank during the day. Nobody was there to supervise me. But I was twenty-four years old, big and bad and all grown-up. Nobody could tell me what I could and couldn't drink.

Well, my body could. And so could the doctors.

After the holidays in '77, I lost a lot of weight and knew something was wrong. Basically I was lying to everybody, telling them I was fine but knowing I wasn't. My father knew something was wrong. One day when I went in to get a checkup, between my leaving the bakery and getting to the doctor's office, my father called and threatened the doctor.

"If you don't put Doug in the hospital, we're going somewhere else," my father said.

Dad knew. I'd lost too much weight. And my father was right. It turned out I had an ulcer in my intestines. There was an inflammation between the small and large intestines, a condition known as Crohn's disease. This was causing the pain in my abdomen and the weight loss. There's no cure for Crohn's disease and it can become life-threatening.

My surgery basically involved removing the portions of my intestines that had been damaged by Crohn's disease. The surgeons then joined together the healthy ends.

After the surgery, I remember waking up and seeing my dad standing at my bedside weeping. I braced myself for the news.

"Dad, if there's something wrong, just tell me."

He wiped his tears and smiled. "Doug, I'm so happy you're going to be okay."

For the two weeks following the fire, my father and I searched through the charred remains of the bakery. There wasn't much that we could salvage: just a few knives and a couple of scales and pans. Neither of us knew if or how we'd be able to continue our business.

Dad was a great baker. I think my dad's business philosophy was if we were busy, then we were making money. I would come to learn early in the business world that *profit* is not a dirty word. I'm not afraid to make a profit. My father was more concerned with keeping the bakery going and keeping employees working than he was with making a profit. Since we lived above the bakery when I was growing up, the overhead and expenses were low and our family did fine.

By the time I got out of high school, our neighborhood had changed and our business had grown. The demographics in our town had shifted as more African Americans were moving south of Chicago to the suburbs. We never had plans to move on, however; the neighborhood was changing but we weren't. We remained busy, especially with our cake business. There were many wedding cakes made during this time. I never remember a time not having meaningful work. We were always busy for six days. We were also always closed on Sundays, without a question.

After the fire, my father gave me some instructions: "Go get a real job."

I worked at two different bakeries while my father went to work for a bakery in a local grocery store. He would end up working there for the next decade. We looked into buying a couple other bakeries and trying to make a go of it, but nothing ever worked out.

During this time, I experienced all the emotions you'd normally go through: stress and wonder and worry and anger. I never questioned my faith in God, however. I might have asked, "God, where are You and what do You have in store for me?" God always answers with a *yes*, *no*, or *let's wait*. I was in a waiting period for a year and a half. God found me good work that I'm thankful for.

I never questioned that God was God. I only questioned what was next.

"Will You provide my daily bread?"

I didn't know where it would come from, but God was faithful. It would always come. My parents raised and protected me when I was young, and now I was in a position where I had to protect Marilyn and Pam. There was never a question of whether I'd be able to do it. I just had to put feet on my faith to move forward through a very difficult time.

Marilyn knew we were going to be okay. Her father passed away at a young age, so she had already endured tough times as a kid. I was Marilyn's rock, and she knew things were going to be good because I was in charge. Even as a young person I instilled confidence in her. Marilyn also believed God would provide for our family. That was all Marilyn was concerned about: our family. She hadn't spent a lot of time in the bakery, so losing it didn't impact her the way it did my father and me. I didn't want it to as well. I was thankful to find work at two other bakeries in the next year even though I probably wasn't a good employee. I struggled to take orders from others.

It turned out the fire had been started by a tenant in the building. I don't know if my father ever pressed charges or if the man was arrested for arson. The fire was very devastating at the time, but looking back on it now, it was a blessing in many ways.

I don't think I grieved the loss of the bakery. I focused on providing for my family, since there was a house payment to make and groceries to buy and bills to pay. I was in survival mode, living in the moment instead of long-term planning. I kept a lot of my emotions inside. During that time, I was able to keep my home life and my professional life separate. Marilyn provided a safe place for our family, so home was an oasis. Everything was good there.

Maybe I was too young to fully fathom what happened with the bakery. I just know I didn't worry because I figured God would provide. And He did.

CHAPTER SEVEN

A New Career

God's amazing grace and my big mouth. That's been one of the major themes of my life. It certainly sums up how I made my transition from baking to steel.

In the spring of 1979, after a short stint at a small beverage company in Chicago, I started working for a manufacturing plant as a serviceman, checking on and fixing some of the equipment they made. It was the beginning of a twenty-two-year career with the company. The change from baking to steel was a blessing I didn't even know at the time.

THE BAKER'S SON

The gentleman who hired me knew I had the ability to present myself and that I was good with my hands. I wasn't super handy, but I had enough self-confidence and could answer questions that customers might have. My job involved repairing some of their equipment and traveling around the country to do that. Eventually I would become the sales manager for the entire Chicago area.

I look back and see my hiring as a minor miracle. Back then they didn't do such extensive background checks, so they never knew about the major surgery I had only thirteen months prior to my hire. It was remarkable that I was able to begin working for them. I applied myself and had a good work ethic, developing a good rapport with the customers. With every opportunity I had with the company, I grew But I never imagined I would end up being there for twenty-two years. At the time, it was a job, providing for my family and affording me various opportunities that came along. One such opportunity was eventually finishing college with the company paying for it.

I never stopped baking, however. The fire might have destroyed our physical property and our business, but it didn't end our desire to continue baking.

Two weeks after the fire, after realizing the business was gone and nothing was left in the ashes, the phones began to start ringing.

"You do not have to make donuts, and you do not have to make bread, but you need to make cakes."

Back in the day, a reception hall would take the order for the cake. "Give me the number 3 serving two hundred people." A cake was part of their package. So we began making cakes for reception halls. Every weekend I'd make three to five cakes. As time went on, I began expanding my efforts to making cakes, cookies, and pastries.

I bought equipment for baking, and little by little this side business grew. I started with a scale, a small mixer, and a fridge. Dad helped me, coming by my house to assist in the baking. This was the beginning of Biegel's Cakery.

I will never forget the first cake we made after the fire. My father came over to my house, and we made a wedding cake on the Ping-Pong table in my basement. I remember my father and I sitting on chairs, looking into the glass on the front of the oven, watching the cake begin to rise. This was the first of many such cakes.

When you start over, you have to start small and make it simple. But God can make anything substantial.

I don't know if I ever really thought of opening up another bakery. At the time, I prayed to God that He'd let me have a little spending money and a little money to help others. That's how I've always felt and how I was raised, wanting to be able to give something to other people and hoping to have some extra money to spend on the family. From day one of baking that first cake, my side business has continued to grow. I've had a regular job that provided for the family, and I've been baking and making what I call the "funny money." The little extra. My hobby supported my bad habits, which, I've joked, was spending money on the children.

My parents taught me how to be generous with my time, my talents, and my money, and to this day I try to do all three of those things. One reason I'm able to help other people is because of what I do in the basement, but the only reason I'm able to be a blessing to others is because of how God has blessed me.

Two amazing blessings were when Amy was born on June 20, 1980, and when Mark was born on April 8, 1983. Our family was growing. God was good.

In 1980, a neighbor across the street from my parents' trailer at Shady Shores said to me, "Doug, you need a place." But there was no way this could happen.

"Pete, I can't afford it."

"Make me an offer," he told me.

I could only offer everything I had at the time. "I only have $2,800."

"It's yours."

So we bought the trailer across from the parents, and it would be ours until 1988, when we sold it and bought another on the same lot we have now.

Gun Lake wasn't just a secondary home we would visit. It was a sanctuary, and our time there was sacred. Oftentimes Marilyn would spend a week at Shady Shores with the family while I went back to work. We chose to raise our children there during the summers. The friends we had back then are still our friends to this day. Marilyn didn't have a car to drive, so I would leave her and the children with thirty dollars for the week.

When I came back, she often had fifteen dollars left over. This became our lives, and they were fun times.

Not once have I ever thought of giving up the place at Gun Lake. Sometimes the drive from Illinois to Michigan has drained me. No, many times it's been a drag making that trip. But just like faith and family and church are nonnegotiables, so is Gun Lake. They were the highlights of the summers, and they are many of the memories I still carry of Marilyn long after she passed away.

Some careers seem natural and you see them coming, like the bakery had been for me. Others are unexpected and last far longer than you think they might. That's how my time at the manufacturing plant proved to be. After a few years there, I enjoyed it and grew in my position. I found myself making more money than I thought human beings should make. In five years I was a service manager who traveled the country. Then I decided to apply for a product manager position that I never thought I'd get, but they hired me for it. Five years after this, another sales opportunity came that I applied for, but I knew I wouldn't get it because I didn't have a college degree. They gave it to me, however, along with paying for me to complete my education.

My job consisted of servicing the company's equipment, so I was always dealing with people. For other manufacturing companies that were using our equipment, I was one of the guys they called. They made products that identified, terminated, and contained electrical wires, items such as labels to identify the wires and the cable ties that bound them together. We also made rings and forks and lugs to terminate the ends of the wires.

I had gone from knowing how to bake cakes and breads and pastries to understanding the electrical world.

It turns out I was born to be a salesperson. "Doug's the name. Selling's my game." I ended up learning that at the bakery. Networking has always been part of my DNA. I value good relationships, and that's one of the blessings I've enjoyed my whole life: good, solid relationships with people. Real relationships, the sort that remain for years, even decades. Even now in the various industries I'm in, I continue to touch base with people I've impacted and who have impacted me.

Paul is one such person who had a great impact on

my life. He was my immediate sales manager. One day when I told him I wanted to move into the job someone had vacated, Paul told me I needed to finish college. I went back for a degree completion program. One year later, Paul left and I was promoted to Chicago district sales manager. I probably talk to Paul two or three times a year, and I always thank him for the impact he's made on my life.

CHAPTER EIGHT

Death

"I know what I'm doing. I have it all planned out—plans to take care of you, not abandon you, plans to give you the future you hope for."

This is what God has told us, what God wants us to believe. But at times in our lives, it's hard to. Sometimes it's downright impossible. There are moments that arrive when the Lord who declared these words in Jeremiah 29:11 seems to be missing and busy. There are events that occur that challenge our faith.

These are the times when our faith can either shine or be shattered.

1978 was one such year. I thought that was tough, watching a family business burst into flames and never get built back up again. But 1985 brought a whole new depth of despair, a sort I could never imagine.

On a fall Saturday in September 1984, I left to deliver a wedding cake, and when I arrived back home, it looked like a million people were there at the house. It turned out Marilyn had gotten gravely sick. She was brought to a doctor, thinking she had the flu, but the doctor wanted her to get X-rays. She ended up going to the hospital and spending the next week there. We learned she had viral cardiomyopathy.

For someone with such a big heart, it turned out this was Marilyn's weakest organ in her body.

Cardiomyopathy is a disease of the heart muscle that makes it harder for the heart to pump blood through the rest of one's body. A virus had attacked her heart, and when Marilyn was diagnosed, we were told the largest percentage of her heart wasn't functioning, and it had been like that for a while. She went to Loyola University Medical Center and they confirmed the diagnosis.

The truth stung.

In my heart of hearts, I realized I probably wouldn't still have Marilyn when I retired. But I never imagined she would die a year later.

In the last year of her life, Marilyn took care of herself while improving. She was doing all the right things, riding her exercise bike and losing weight all while raising three children. Our family went to Florida for spring break that year. On our ten-year anniversary on July 19, 1985, we were able to get away to northern Michigan, leaving the children with my family while we took a vacation. It had been a great year.

On September 11, 1985, I came home late from work. Marilyn had invited my parents over for dinner, which wasn't unusual, and had spent a couple of hours talking to her sister. Around bedtime, she told me she was a little cold; we usually slept with our window open, so I said I'd close it.

The next morning, I woke up at my normal time and took a shower. When I kissed Marilyn goodbye like

I always did, I noticed that she felt a little cold. By the time I stepped into the garage about to leave for work, I couldn't shake a thought about her.

She never moved over to the warm spot in our bed.

I went back inside to check on Marilyn, and when I tried to nudge her awake, I realized she was gone.

Sometime during the night, Marilyn had passed away.

A panic filled me as life suddenly went on pause while I freaked out trying to figure out what to do. I immediately called Joy, my sister.

"It's Marilyn. Something's wrong."

"I'll call the paramedics," Joy said. "You just take care of the children."

The children . . .

Eight-year-old Pam.

Five-year-old Amy.

And two-year-old Mark.

I tried to keep the children away from everything, explaining why strangers were about to start coming into our house.

"Mommy's sick," I told them. "She's got to go to the hospital."

The paramedics were the first to arrive, and the

very first one was a guy I knew. When the whole group came, they had one paramedic staying with me the entire time. I was able to tell them what medications she took and when she took them. I explained how she had been feeling fine and how she'd told me before bed that she felt a little cold. When they asked me about her Social Security number, I lost it.

"What the hell difference does it make what her Social Security number is? Just get her to the hospital."

While I was talking to the paramedic, the rest of them were in the other room working on Marilyn. I heard a loud boom but didn't know where it came from. Five minutes later, when I heard the noise again, I realized they were shocking her, trying to revive her heart with a defibrillator. Even though she passed at home, the protocol in Illinois with the paramedics is they have to attempt to revive the patient and are required to take them to the hospital. They pronounced her dead at the hospital.

Marilyn was twenty-nine years old, less than a month away from her thirtieth birthday. I was thirty-two. She had been doing so well, yet her heart simply gave out on her. The doctor said she had the heart of an eighty-year-old woman.

THE BAKER'S SON

Every momentous occasion in life calls for a cake. A birthday, a wedding, a funeral. So it doesn't surprise me that a day after my wife Marilyn passed away, I was making a cake. This wasn't for the wake and the funeral; it was for a wedding. It's the most difficult cake I've ever made in my life.

Marilyn passed away on a Thursday, and on Friday night we had her wake. It was an amazing experience. Our daughter Amy didn't want to go to the wake and funeral, and I didn't make her. On Saturday, we would be having her funeral at our church. It just so happened that John and Laurel were getting married on the same day in the same church. John left his wedding rehearsal to come to Marilyn's wake. While we were talking, he asked me to do something for him.

"I don't want you to make our wedding cake," he told me.

"John . . . I am going to make that wedding cake if it's filled with tears and if it's the last cake I ever make. There will be a cake at your wedding from Biegel's Cakery."

I made that cake, and my father and brother-in-law,

Gary, delivered it to the wedding. Just hours after my friend John got married, my wife who was from the same church was buried.

After a beautiful funeral, our family and friends were inside the church sharing a meal. The woman taking care of Amy ended up bringing her to church, so when she stepped into the hall, it wiped out a lot of people and brought many to tears. To this day, Amy has a hard time going to funerals.

Pam was there, but I don't remember if Mark was at the funeral. What tears me up today is to see our grandchildren and to see the ages our three kids were at when Marilyn passed away. Eight, five, and two.

So young, so little.

It hurts sometimes to see Mark's children, Zeke and Nina, and to remember how young he was when his mother died. His *first* mother. A mother he never knew, one he only remembers from photos and stories.

Debbie is the only mom Mark has ever known.

After Marilyn passed away, Pam said she thought she had to be the one to worry in our family. She assumed this because I've never been one to share my worries or put them on others.

"Pam, I'm the parent. God gave me this gift. I'll do the worrying. You be a child and have fun."

When Billy Graham spoke at the crusade where I gave my life to Christ, I remember him talking about God.

"He knows what you face," Graham said as if he were speaking only to me. "There's never been a problem that you've ever faced that Jesus hasn't been there. Death? He's been there. Trouble? He's been there. Temptation that you can't seemingly resist? He's felt the same temptation."

God knew how I felt and what I was going through. And I'll be honest. Losing Marilyn was tough. Really tough. I knew we wouldn't have her for long, but I never thought she'd die that young.

It was awful. But even in her death, God was faithful.

At Marilyn's funeral, someone shared Jeremiah 29:11 with me, the verse I started this chapter with. This became my life verse.

I know what I'm doing, Doug. I have it all planned out—plans to take care of you and your family, not abandon you, plans to give you the future you and your children hope for.

I'm thankful for God's faithfulness. With each passing day, I grow more thankful.

None of us is promised tomorrow, and none of us can change yesterday. All we have is today.

CHAPTER NINE

Grief

God is good, and God is faithful. Through the good times and the bad.

Losing a spouse and a loved one is overwhelming and all-consuming. I did the best I could to carry on with life. *These kids need to be at school,* I reminded myself. *They need to be at church.* I needed to let others know that God was being faithful to us even during this difficult time.

On the Sunday morning after Marilyn's death, I

brought the children to church. A woman in the balcony would later tell me she was astonished to see our family sitting down below her in the pew. Marilyn, their mother, died on Thursday. Yet there we sat the following Sunday morning at church. The woman above us began to weep, and she eventually needed to leave because her tears wouldn't stop.

I wasn't trying to be noble or some kind of saint. This was simply where our family needed to be, where I needed to be. At Thorn Creek Reformed Church, around people who loved Jesus and who loved our family. Anger at a time like this was normal, but I knew that God was good.

This situation isn't good for you now, Doug, but God is good. Never forget that.

I never questioned God during this time. Yes, I certainly missed Marilyn, but I was grateful the children didn't have to see her suffering. I knew from day one that Marilyn was walking streets of gold, that God had built her a home by the crystal sea. She was much better off. So I didn't question my heavenly Father. I simply did the best I could to carry on with life.

During those months, I found myself in survival mode, worried about what we would have for supper the following day and wondering who would come watch the kids after school. It's difficult to grieve for someone when you're simply trying to get through the day. I had to fill the role of a father and a mother. Single-parenting is the most difficult time of someone's life, regardless of how they might have gotten to this point.

Here's the truth: people don't know what to say to you after a tragedy like this, so they avoid you at church or anywhere. I used to sit in the kitchen at night and stare at the phone, praying to God that someone would call me so I could have a grown-up conversation. "Please, God, just let somebody call." I needed to talk to someone other than my mother and my father.

I'm thankful for all the help I received. My parents came every morning to make the children breakfast, while Joy and Gary came over on Sundays to do the girls' hair before church. Many, many people invited us out to dinner, and I wasn't too proud to turn them down. Since the children were little, we weren't required to stay long. I always had family and friends around to support me, and I wasn't afraid to ask for help. I could afford a lot of things, such as buying new dresses for our daughters for Easter, yet I didn't always know how to do things like picking the right outfit. That's when I'd call my female friends and ask for support. Many neighbors helped me; two of our neighbors would brush our girls' hair, for instance.

Growing up, I'd been taught to extend a helping hand to someone in need. Now it was my time to accept that from others, to be a recipient. I was a little proud at first, but I got over that quickly. I knew I needed help and was in a bad spot.

Two months after Marilyn died, Amy asked me to come to the Pilgrims' Day celebration in her kindergarten class. With Thanksgiving approaching, all the parents were invited to come visit their child's classroom. Amy wanted me to come, so I showed up and realized I was the only father there. I didn't show any emotions during my time with the class as we watched all the kids put their cans of soup together. After I left the classroom and was safely in the comfort of my car, I lost it.

There were many tears shed in the sanctuary of my car during this time.

I've always spent a lot of time in my car as part of my job, so it was natural to have lots of meltdowns in there. Early on after Marilyn died, I'd end up having to leave work early on a Friday a few times. I was physically, emotionally, and mentally spent. I frequently called my mom when I was coming home. She often would have Neal Ausema come to my house ten minutes after I got home. Neal was a godly man whose wife was killed in a horrific car wreck. He understood the pain I was going through. Neal remarried and eventually he and his wife became close friends to Debbie and me.

Neal would always be there for me, someone I could express my frustration and anger and disappointment with. This older gentleman just watched me cry until the kids got home from school. I didn't let them know how bad I was hurting; I didn't want them to see my tears. But Neal saw them. Neal understood. He spent a lot of time simply listening to me, standing and sitting next to me and hearing my pain. It was so good to have him and other great friends I could call on my bad days to talk about Marilyn. I needed to talk about her, and obviously I didn't want to burden the children about it. I never did that with them, nor did I share these things when I began to date Debbie.

Marilyn's death was hard. I tried to remain positive for the kids, hiding my pain from them. Sometimes when life became too overwhelming, I would go to the cemetery and spend some solitary time at Marilyn's grave site. I put on a good front to her, too.

THE BAKER'S SON

"The children are fine. I'm fine. It's all good."

By the end of the year, things weren't good. *I* was not doing well. I finally reached my breaking point. Something needed to change.

I spent New Year's Eve alone with the children. After taking down the Christmas tree, the kids told me they wanted a pizza. It was ten o'clock at night, and I didn't know if any shops were still open. I called a bunch of places, but nobody answered. So being the good father that I was, I decided to go out and drive around in search of some pizza. Being the bad parent that I was, I left the kids home alone.

After driving around and searching for a while only to discover every single pizza place in Illinois closed for New Year's Eve, my anger and frustration inside boiled over. I had a complete meltdown.

"I can't do this, God," I cried out.

My children wanted a pizza and I couldn't find one for them. What sort of father was I? I needed more help. I needed more time. I needed a wife, a mate, a partner.

"I just can't do this alone."

The car I rode around in resembled my life. I was

driving all around by myself with the windows rolled up, keeping all the pain and anger and questions and anxiety inside, away from the kids.

This night wasn't just a breaking point. It marked the moment of change, when I realized that I needed to change.

Enough's enough, Doug. We're going to move on.

For the sake of my kids and my family and friends and myself, I needed to have faith in Jeremiah 29:11 and move on.

I didn't need God to tell me what to do next. If you keep reading in Jeremiah 29, God gives us instructions on how to deal with the good times and the bad ones.

Doug, when you call on me, when you come and pray to me, I'll listen.

I needed to come before the Lord and not only pray. I needed to listen.

Doug, when you come looking for me, you'll find me.

I was looking for a pizza, but really I was searching for something else. For someone else.

Yes, Doug, when you get serious about finding me and want it more than anything else, I'll make sure you won't be disappointed.

I was more than serious. I needed God more than

ever. I had the help of others around me, but what I really needed was the hope God brings.

Doug, I'll turn things around for you. I'll . . . bring you home to the place from which I sent you off into exile. You can count on it.

To this day, people call me on the date Marilyn passed away. It's such a blessing. She's gone but not forgotten.

Whenever we get together as a family, I just hope God opens heaven's window a little bit and lets Marilyn see that these kids have turned out so well and that these grandkids are good.

There's something I've told people on their deathbed.

"When you get to heaven and see Marilyn, tell her we're fine. Tell her the kids are good."

That's what I want Marilyn to know. The children are good. All of our children have turned out remarkable.

I also want Marilyn to know that God brought me two amazing and godly women who love God and their family and their church. It took losing one to find the other.

CHAPTER TEN

Starting Over

Debbie was there for me from day one.

I say this partially tongue in cheek, but I firmly believe it's true. It's because the very first sympathy card I ever received was from Debbie; I remember that to this day. She might argue with that, but that's my recollection. Whether it was the first actual card I opened, I don't know, but I do know it's the first one I remember.

Debbie was my next-door neighbor's granddaughter. Just saying that might raise a few eyebrows.

Bert and Ada Voss lived next door to our family. Every Sunday we had to go to their house for coffee; it was a religious event. Bert and Ada treated us like we were their children. I remember I had a baby Moses basket that carried our kids home from the hospital. In April of '83, we brought Mark home on a Sunday; in fact, I think all my kids came home on a Sunday. Marilyn and I walked into Bert and Ada's house with this new baby, and the entire family including Debbie was there. I remember seeing twenty-four-year-old Debbie and wondering why she was still single. They often had the entire family at their house on Sundays, and this is when I would see Debbie.

A funny story. Bert chain-smoked Camel unfiltered cigarettes off his fingertips, and even though he smoked inside, their house never smelled like cigarettes. I don't know how Grandma did it. Every time we brought a child home from the hospital, Bert was sitting in his chair and I put the newborn in his arms. He was so nervous that he decided to light one of those Camels.

"Bert," I said, "it's a brand-new baby. You can't be blowing smoke at the baby."

Debbie Meter was the eldest of five siblings, and her family went to Marilyn's family's church. Debbie had gone to grade school and high school with Marilyn's sister Elaine, so we not only knew her grandparents but we knew the Meter family as well. So a sympathy card from Debbie wouldn't have seemed like it came out of the blue. But I did take notice of it.

After receiving a Christmas card from Debbie, I decided to call her and ask if she wanted to go to an Oak Ridge Boys concert that was taking place on New Year's Eve. Yes, *that* New Year's Eve when I had my breakdown and epiphany. I didn't even have tickets and didn't know how I'd get them. I learned later that Debbie's sister, Lori, happened to be at her parents' house when I asked her to this concert, and she was more excited than Debbie.

"Debbie, he's got kids!" Lori said. "And he's got a summer home! Don't let him go!"

Debbie was gracious when she turned me down, saying she had plans. I didn't need to worry about getting those tickets after all. Maybe I needed to spend time by myself on New Year's Eve. Maybe God knew I needed to fall apart in order to stand back up and start moving ahead. That's exactly what I did in the New Year. It started a couple weeks into January 1986.

THE BAKER'S SON

I'm in the basement in the laundry room with the door closed. The kids are upstairs in bed while I'm sitting on a chair holding the receiver of a corded phone. My knees are knocking, my palms are sweating, and my hands are shaking as I start to dial Debbie's number.

I'm thirty-two years old and asking a girl out on a date.

I don't want to start this again.

I struck out the first time with the Oak Ridge Boys. Now I'm asking her to go to a boat show with me. Debbie says yes.

My life changes in that moment with that decision.

As we walk through the aisles at the McCormick Place looking at all these boats that are way out of my league, I feel like a nervous wreck while Debbie looks beautiful. I haven't done this sort of thing in years, so I question every step. Like where do you go for a meal? Since I'm a sensitive guy, I don't want to offend her in any way, so I take her to Fuddruckers in Calumet City just to be safe.

I don't talk about Marilyn on our first date. It's a subject I will broach carefully, and it's also a topic we won't talk about a lot over the years. If there's any elephant in the room as we get to know each other, it's the children. They are an important part of my life. I'm blessed to discover that they become an important part of Debbie's life as well.

Debbie doesn't act nervous on our first date. I think she's happy to be going out on a date, happy to have someone interested in her. I come to discover that she has not dated very much over the years, and she is quite guarded with her feelings. I say that if you become a garden friend of Debbie, you're the exception and not the rule. This is the sort of friend you take into your garden and show them all your "stuff." You take only really close friends into your garden. You can take people into your home, but to bring them into your garden is another step up.

A new story begins; in a lot of ways, a whole new life starts to unfold.

God is faithful.

The only ones who knew about that first date were Debbie's parents. Of course I eventually told the kids I was seeing Debbie, but we kept our relationship on the

DL because I couldn't tell her grandparents. I would perch each of the kids at a different window to spy on Debbie as she walked into her grandparents' house.

For our first few dates, we tried to go outside of our community. Debbie was driving the bus for Elim Christian School, and sometimes I would get the children up early and ready in order to meet her on the morning route. Once a week Debbie came over to make dinner, and she stopped by after church volleyball games.

Debbie and I had a lot of fun. It was tough being a single parent, working, and dating, all while trying to let Debbie know this was normal. We did a lot, just the two of us, and I tried to include the children so she would realize what she potentially was getting herself into. As a family, it was something we had to navigate and work out. To this day, I'm amazed that my kids have turned out so well because they've been shipped from pillar to post. I didn't exclude them. It wasn't long after we started dating, two or three months, that Debbie's mother would have us over on Sunday for lunch, so I always brought the kids.

One day when Debbie's high school had a game against mine, she told me she wanted to go.

"I'm willing to go, but you realize it's going to get a lot of people talking," I told her.

We went to the game and the rest is history.

CHAPTER ELEVEN

Someone to Love

When Debbie and I arrived at Shady Shores at Gun Lake on Memorial Day of '86, it's safe to say that we received some looks. *A lot* of looks. The last time everybody on Fir Lane saw me, Marilyn and I were packing up the cottage on Labor Day to go home. Ten days later she was dead. Now I was coming back the following spring with this new young lady.

That first night we pulled up to the small trailer with three bedrooms, then put the kids to bed and didn't know what to do. We finally pulled down the shades. In some ways, it didn't matter what we were doing. People could think what they wanted to think and say what they wanted to say.

Very few people could understand the road I had traveled since leaving the lake nine months ago. They didn't realize the truth about Doug Biegel's heart.

I need to be in fellowship with people. I need help at home. But most of all I need someone to love and to help me in this journey of life.

I found a love and a life in Debra Lee Meter.

I understood the looks we received and some of the ludicrous things we heard. But here's the truth. Head knowledge and experiential knowledge are two hugely different things. I can tell you that a heart surgery hurts, but until you've actually experienced a heart surgery, you don't realize how much it hurts. It's the same thing with losing a spouse. And it's one of the ironic blessings in my life, because I can go up to people and not only say, "I feel bad for you," but I can truly identify with people who have lost a spouse.

"My heart was broken just like yours," I tell them. "I know how it feels because I've experienced it."

I've told this to a lot of people: you have no idea

until you walk in those shoes. I've told children whose parents are about to remarry, grown kids who don't want another mom or another dad, to please love on your parents. Love and accept them because you have no idea.

From the first moment Debbie sneezed that first night at Shady Shores, she had to endure a horrible summer of allergies at the lake. For three months she walked around carrying a box of Kleenex. One reason is that the trailer we were in didn't have cement underneath it. It's a blessing and a miracle that Debbie never gave up on the lake. To this day, she loves Shady Shores and all the people there. Thank You, Lord. That was another God thing. One more on a long list.

I'm not sure what I would have done if Debbie didn't want to be at the lake. I was willing to make a lot of changes, but giving up Shady Shores and the lake wasn't one of them.

We were the talk of Shady Shores. Actually, Debbie and I were the talk of the greater South Holland area. It was pretty amusing. I don't want to sugarcoat things; there were some tough times. Many people in our lives were happy for us, and people I knew were happy I was dating. I didn't take a survey of who approved and who didn't; I really didn't care. What I cared about was this woman I was getting to know.

I discovered that Debbie was a diamond in the rough. As the oldest of five children, she grew up in a good family with two loving parents. By the time I met her, Debbie was struggling with self-esteem and why she was still single. We had a discussion once about this.

"Why have I been alone for so long?" Debbie said.

"Debbie, God was saving you for me. God kept you single for a reason. He had plans for us."

As we dated that summer, the children adjusted easily. The Meters had a built-in swimming pool, so the kids were going to Gun Lake on the weekends and then going to Grandma Meter's on Thursdays and Fridays. Debbie became a weekend mommy.

For the first few months of dating, when Debbie came over to the house, I would take down all the pictures of Marilyn; then I would put them back up so the kids didn't notice in the morning. After doing this for a while, I eventually said *Enough of this* and left them where they were. I tried to make sure Debbie knew the only thing she and Marilyn had in common was that they're both women. Other than that, they are two different people. I explained this early on in our relationship.

"I will never compare you," I told Debbie. "I will never say, 'She made this' and 'Will you make this for me?'"

I tried then and I still try to always make Debbie feel special. The further down the road we've come, the more we can talk about this experience. Writing this book has been one of those opportunities to allow this to happen.

In August of that year, Debbie and I flew to Florida to stay with her aunt Sharon and uncle Junie. I booked Pam and Amy on a flight to Seattle to stay with their aunt Ann and uncle Ralph and cousins, while Mark stayed with one of Marilyn's brothers and his wife, Tom and Jeanne. Debbie couldn't believe I'd do something like that, especially since we weren't even engaged yet.

The trip was surreal for me. There we were, thirteen months after Marilyn's death, staying with Debbie's aunt and uncle. I was still pretty physically, emotionally, and mentally drained. Sharon and Junie had a pool at their place, so I would sit by the water for six or seven hours a day, and they thought something was wrong with me.

"He's just tired," Debbie explained to them.

We had a great time. But we weren't official yet. We needed to cross some hurdles before tying the knot.

In those early days of dating, Debbie questioned what she was getting into. At one point she even decided it was too much. I never gave up on her.

We had gone shopping one night for a television since I needed a new one. I asked Debbie to accompany me, because truthfully I wanted her to make a decision. Little did I know this wasn't her strong suit. While looking, I put her on the spot.

"So which one do you want? Do you want this one or that one?"

Which one do you want? I didn't understand how loaded the word *you* could be. My comment had been the straw that broke the camel's back. The one that finally told Debbie the truth.

This is for real, Debbie.

That was the night she dumped me.

I think until that moment, she thought she could exit this relationship at anytime. She never said that, but I think there were no tangible things that were going to hold us together. So this television was the first thing that was going to hold us together.

A couple days later, I woke up the kids really early.

"Hey, we need to go see Debbie and bring her some coffee and donuts."

Somehow I managed to break into the garage where her bus was parked. We waited in there to surprise her, and surprise her we did. I think she was pretty irritated with me for being there.

"I don't believe this," she said. "I thought we were done."

I did not want to let her go. I could tell she was annoyed I was there and had even brought the kids, so all I could do was smile and share with her a donut and a cup of coffee.

"Have a good day," I told her.

Thankfully, we weren't done.

One night after dinner when the kids were in bed, I told Debbie everything was going to be okay. Then we read Proverbs 3:5-6:

> "Trust in the Lord with all your heart,
>   and lean not on your own understanding;

in all your ways acknowledge Him
and He will direct your paths."

Late that fall, Debbie and I took a ride to the Covered Bridge Festival in Indiana. We hit some craft sales but only found one bridge. On the way back home, we stopped at a restaurant for dinner. I ended up asking Debbie to marry me.

"I hoped we would make it back in time to go to downtown Chicago so I could propose," I told her. "But I couldn't wait."

Shortly after this, it was time to tell the kids. I decided to do it at the house one night after dinner. Debbie was coming over once or twice a week, arriving after work to cook supper for us and help put the kids to bed. Oftentimes after dinner we played games with the kids. We were playing the game of Life on the kitchen table, and Debbie passed the "Getting Married" space. The rules are a person is supposed to stop even if they have moves left, then take one Life Tile and add one person peg to the car. Then they're supposed to spin and move again. As Debbie went to spin for prizes, I put my hand on hers and stopped her.

"Debbie, you know that you have to get engaged before you get married and start a family," I said.

I pulled an engagement ring out of my shirt pocket and asked her to marry me. Debbie couldn't believe we had kept the secret from her during dinner. Thankfully, she said yes.

We never finished the game. Instead, we decided to live it out.

Debbie was already part of another family. I want to say a few words about this amazing family.

Marilyn's family never left me and always included Debbie as part of their family. To this day the Venhuizens still include us with everything. We try to always get together with them around the holidays, and for that I'm grateful. Every one of Marilyn's siblings counts Debbie as a family member. My mother-in-law, Mrs. Venhuizen, counted our children together as her own grandchildren. There was never any differentiation. Never in any way.

It is amazing.

Every time we leave a Venhuizen gathering, I thank Debbie for being willing to go there and be with them.

"Doug, I know those people."

Debbie's been around them for over thirty-three years now. She can laugh at their stories of when they were kids because she's heard these stories for thirty-three years. But it doesn't change the fact that it is an amazing thing.

How good is God?

How gracious is His love?

CHAPTER TWELVE

A New Life Together

"We are getting married!"

The announcement being made to the staff at the Glenwood Oaks banquet hall wasn't shouted by me but rather by four-year-old Mark. It was June 27, 1987, and our son was excited for the upcoming wedding. But before Debbie and I could say our vows, I had to deliver our wedding cake.

By the time the service took place at eleven in the morning, Cottage Grove Christian Reformed Church was packed. All of the kids were excited to be standing up in the wedding. Pam was ten and Amy was seven. A very jubilant Mark was exhausted from being woken up early that day, so during the ceremony he fell asleep on the stairs.

The Bible verse Debbie and I chose from Proverbs 3:5-6 is one that we've lived by ever since:

> Trust in the Lord with all your heart,
>   and lean not on your own understanding;
> in all your ways acknowledge Him,
>   and He will direct your paths.

As we said our vows before God and our family and friends, Debbie and I were trusting the Lord and submitting to Him. We didn't have everything figured out; there were still lots of questions in both of our hearts and minds. But we were proclaiming a life with one another and promising to be by each other's side through life's joys and sorrows.

This was Debbie's special day, and so much of the joy I experienced came from watching her. The children surprised Debbie with two songs at the reception they learned from her mother: "Welcome to the Family" and

"Bicycle Built for Two." After the afternoon reception, we ended up going to Debbie's parents' house to have a pool party.

We were starting our married life together. For me in many ways, I was starting over. When it came to where we were going to live, I asked Debbie before the wedding what she wanted to do.

"Debbie, you have two choices. You can remodel and expand this house any way you want, or we can move."

By that time, my house was almost paid for.

"I want to move," Debbie said, explaining that she didn't want to live next to her grandparents, and that she wanted to start our life together with a clean slate.

We knew we would stay in South Holland and the kids would stay at Calvin Christian School. We looked at quite a few homes, eventually deciding on the one on University Avenue, south of Dick James Ford. For a few months before we got married, Debbie had fun decorating it and getting the house ready for me and the kids to move in. I took very little from the house I had, instead giving much of it away. Those were just things; nothing could take away the memories our family had made in that house.

For our honeymoon, Debbie and I traveled to San Diego for a week and a half, spending July 4 at Disneyland. When we arrived back home, we took the kids camping at Turkey Run State Park in Indiana, where we stayed at the lodge. We included the kids in our honeymoon because all of us were starting a new life together.

I was married twice in the same church and got a blessing from the council both times, but no blessing in life comes without bumps or stumbling blocks. There were challenges early on with our marriage, ones that would have come with any father of three young children marrying again. We were able to find a Christian counselor, and she was a huge help to all of us.

There were others who helped us as well. Neal and Laverne Ausema were an older couple who were so good to Debbie and me. We would go to their house after church on Sundays just to visit them, even on those days when life wasn't so peachy and rosy. They always listened to us, and they would pray with us and be encouraging.

There were a few more meltdowns I had in the

privacy of my car. Times when I would have to call a friend and just admit how much I was hurting. To open up and ask how I could still have feelings for Marilyn when I was now married to Debbie.

"Doug, you loved Marilyn," my friend said. "Just because she died didn't mean you stopped loving her."

Proverbs 3:5-6 definitely showed us the road we needed to take. Trusting in the Lord instead of ourselves, and submitting to His ways in order to know the right path.

God blessed our family on January 9, 1989, when Jana Lee was born. Then on June 22, 1992, Paul Joseph came along. All of a sudden my quiver was full with five beautiful children. Debbie and I were busy, in love and glad to be raising these children.

I've realized over the years that I haven't talked to my kids a lot about Marilyn. As they became adults, it's something I've done more over the phone. During a recent conversation, one of our children opened up to me about Marilyn's death.

"I just want to ask God why."

While I don't know that answer, I do know the remarkable job Debbie has done with our kids. It's truly been a blessing. The older grandkids realize that there is Grandma Marilyn in heaven and Grandma Debbie alive and well. Today I can talk to them about Marilyn without becoming emotional.

Debbie and I have spent thirty-three years together, building a life and a family. I can't imagine my life without her. She is a living and breathing reminder of Lamentations 3:22-23: "The steadfast love of the Lord never ceases; his mercies never come to an end; they are new every morning; great is your faithfulness."

CHAPTER THIRTEEN

Figuring Out Fatherhood

"Remember whose you are."

This is what I always told our children every time they walked out of our house.

"Remember whose you are," I called out to them before they left.

Their friends would sometimes ask what I meant.

"My dad's saying I'm God's child and I'm Doug's child," they would tell their friends.

That's exactly what they are. God's child and Doug's child. And I reminded them that even though Doug couldn't see them, God always could.

When I think of our five children and our ten grandchildren now in 2021, I'm overwhelmed with gratitude to God and I thank Him all the time.

Thank You, God, for these kids. Thank You for who they are.

My journey into parenting began as a kid living above the bakery. I saw my father every day on his feet working to provide for our family, and I grew up with an unbelievable respect for him. Joseph Biegel led by example; he never asked anybody to do something he wouldn't do.

When I think of my father, I think of the three most important things in his life: faith, family, and church. As I've already said, if it wasn't one of those three things, my dad didn't want to do it. These were three nonnegotiables in life that my father lived by, and those soon became nonnegotiables for me, too.

My father lived during the Great Depression, so he knew how to work and taught me that as well. He was a workaholic but the only example I saw. That's probably why I like to work as well. I can admit I'm a borderline workaholic myself. I've taught my children the value of hard work, and I can see today how they aren't afraid to step up and volunteer.

As a father, I had three rules for my children:

1. Tell me where you're at.
2. Tell me who you're with.
3. Tell me what time you'll be home.

If any of those things changed, it was their responsibility to get ahold of me. I always made it clear they could call me anytime for anything.

"If you're ever in a position you don't want to be in," I told my children, "you can call me and tell me you're sick and I'll come and pick you up. No questions asked."

We went through beepers and early cell phones. I consider myself fortunate to not have had to parent with smartphones and social media. I wouldn't call myself a disciplinarian; I think I was a work in progress. Looking back, I was probably a little too rough on my older kids, and they'll all admit that Paul got away with murder. By the time our youngest came, if it wasn't illegal or immoral or unethical, I would ask him, "How much does it cost?" and then give him the money. Hey—I was tired by the time Paul came around!

I look at our children and find myself so thankful. I sometimes wonder how God blessed me with five children and not one of them has given me even fifteen seconds' worth of heartache.

Is there some secret to having good kids? If I knew the answer to that, I'd bottle it and sell it. I just know that it's something we can't always talk about with other friends. My mother-in-law taught me not to brag about my children. Instead, I take joy in hearing others praise them. Anytime I hear someone saying, "Let me tell you what your son/daughter did," I take an immense pride in this. Once again, I thank God for our kids and for who they are.

One thing that I have always known: make sure your children have good friends. Easier said than done. I never told my children about their friends I didn't like, but rather I'd say they could make better choices than some of those kids they were around.

As a family, we always sat down for dinner, praying before the meal and then afterward taking the time to read the Bible and pray again. I always did the dishes with our kids when they were young.

My children have seen a father and a mother who walk the walk and talk the talk. Years ago when the kids were young, I was installing a new oven in our basement for the bakery. I ran into a mechanic at the time who was out of work and his back was against the wall, so I had him come over every night for two or three weeks to work on the oven and make some money. To this day, if I call this man and ask him what he remembers from that experience in the nineties, he will say how he had never seen a family that prayed together and ate together and read the Bible together. That was the one thing that meant the most to him, watching our family doing this. The family dinner hour has always been a sacred time and remains that way.

In 1989, we ended up selling the trailer we were in at Gun Lake and putting a new double-wide in a bigger space in the location we're still at now. It was a little farther from the lake but we definitely needed more room.

I marvel when I look back at my children. Nobody ever complained about going to the lake, and nothing interfered with our time there. All of our kids played baseball or softball, but I don't remember many commitments on the weekend preventing us from heading to Michigan. The schedule remained the same as the one I had when I was a teen: always leaving work and spending the weekend at Gun Lake. It became the routine and Debbie fell in love with it just like I did. It's been a phenomenal place to raise our kids.

Family has always been first for me my whole life. I've poured myself into these children for the last forty-plus years. It's natural as a parent to want to comfort them when they're little, and to nurture them even more after they lost their mother. The difficult part in life when you get older is wondering what you're supposed to do with your free time now that the children are all grown up with their own families.

On a recent family trip, our children drove us all the way down to Florida, and I didn't have to clean one dish or make one meal the entire week we were there. They were constantly telling me, "Dad, I got that for you" and, "Dad, can I get a plate for you?"

It's humbling having children like that. When I see how hard they work, I sometimes feel guilty. But then I'm reminded of how hard we've worked as parents and all the lessons we've tried to teach them along the way.

CHAPTER FOURTEEN

A Box Full of Dilly Bars

Sometimes you're sitting next to a stranger in a doctor's office waiting for your name to be called, or you're talking to a server at a restaurant just before she takes your order. All it takes is someone's curiosity to share your story.

One day as I walked into a car dealership carrying an order for cookies, a woman looked at me and asked if I had made all of them.

"Yes, ma'am. Biegel's Cakery. I make handmade pastries from my family's one-hundred-year-old recipes. All our products are made without any preservatives. Our main pastries are banket and fruit-filled strudel."

This is something I've learned as a salesperson, something basic you learn in Sales 101. You have to be able to sell your product in an elevator ride. You have to know the features, advantages, and benefits of your product, and you have to be able to share them in a concise amount of time because most people will only give you a limited amount of time.

If you spend much time around me, you're going to eventually hear mine, and if you've read this far in this book, then you know it well. How in ten months, I bought my first home, had my first child, had four feet of my intestines removed, and lost my family business to fire. That was bad. Seven and a half years later, I woke up and found my wife, Marilyn, dead in bed. That was really bad. But God has been faithful in the good times and the hard times.

When I reached my late forties, I recognized I needed to able to share my own life story in this short amount of time, too. I began to feel quite restless, sensing there was more God wanted me to do, searching for different ways to impact people. By that time in my life, I realized people couldn't fire me for talking about Jesus. I was willing to share my story to anybody who would listen. I've always been a confident person, but in my late forties I developed what I call a holy boldness after realizing what really mattered in life.

All that matters is the impact I'll have on people and how I'll represent Jesus Christ.

Some days, however, I wondered how much of an impact I was really having with my job. One day I shared with Debbie how I felt.

"I'm sick and tired of driving around in a car impacting my windshield."

I felt God nudging me when my manufacturing company held a twentieth anniversary party for me at a restaurant in 1999. It was fun to look back on the past twenty years. The night was full of joy and laughter. It was Debbie's idea to have an open mike and ask my fellow coworkers to share the impact Doug Biegel had had on their lives. The comments were humbling and inspiring. Many of them said they were impacted simply by what I did and the way I lived my life.

After two decades at the same company, I was working as the district sales manager and felt I needed a change. I began to explore what options might be available and found one with one of my customers who was selling his business. They manufactured electrical cable assemblies for boiler companies, and our company had been making all the electrical wiring that made the portable air compressors run. After doing my due diligence, things were all set in place to make the purchase. I had a bank ready to loan me one million dollars. Before I went through with this, I decided it might be wise to go in and see a doctor to get a checkup. It was a good decision, because the doctor told me my blood pressure was elevated and suggested I go to the hospital to get it under control.

It turns out my blood pressure wasn't just elevated; it was off the charts. In fact, a year later my cardiologist would tell me that my blood pressure was over three hundred and that he didn't think I'd make it through the night.

I spent ten days in the hospital after being diagnosed with uncontrolled asymptomatic hypertension and cardiomyopathy. The only word I understood was *uncontrolled.* In layman's terms, I had congestive heart failure. My family knew that cardiomyopathy meant death, and they all freaked out. Once again God showed

His faithfulness. He had a plan for me, and He was not finished with me yet.

To make matters worse, later that year, I would also be diagnosed with sleep apnea, a sleep disorder where breathing repeatedly stops and starts. To this day I sleep with a breathing machine in order to control my oxygen.

Looking back, I'm sure my health issues were from the natural stresses of life. We were raising five children in a blended family and putting all of them through a private school. I'm a workaholic, so work has always been a priority. I'm a big guy and was taught to handle stress by continuing on. It's called life, and you have to deal with it.

Sometimes life can take more of a toll on you than you might imagine.

My plans for buying a company ended while I focused on my health. God had a plan, however. I've said that before, haven't I? Little did I know this plan included a drug I started taking to treat my heart failure. I would come to learn a lot about this medication called Coreg.

In January 2002, with my health now improved, I took a leap of faith and left the manufacturing company for a sales job at a large pharmaceutical company. God was faithful because at that time, I couldn't even spell *pharmaceutical*. I didn't know the first thing about medicine, and the only science class I took was freshman biology at Chicago Christian High School. Four years of high school and another four of college, and I only had one science class. So how in the world did I become a salesperson with a territory close to my house for a major pharmaceutical company?

God's amazing grace and my big mouth.

There were, of course, some natural reasons why I chose this industry. First off, one of my friends and coworkers had left our manufacturing company to become a rep in pharma, and he kept telling me I had to do the same. "You gotta do this, Doug. You gotta do this." So I decided to apply myself and I was hired. I ended up going around the country selling Coreg, the medication that helped save my life. I became a walking and talking testimony for what this medicine could do.

Whenever I spoke to doctors, I would end my speech in the same way. I started by showing them a photograph of my daughters at their weddings.

"My daughters don't ask me how much this medicine costs," I would say. "The value of the medicine is

A BOX FULL OF DILLY BARS

that I was able to walk them down the aisle. The products that you and I carry in our cases every day help people do more, feel better, and live longer."

Usually this brought a standing ovation to my speech. I wasn't making this story up. I was living proof that these medications could impact and save lives.

Not everybody applauded my decision to leave the manufacturing company I'd spent the last twenty-two years at. My father thought I was crazy, asking me why I would make such a change. I saw it as my holy boldness. This desire to make an impact on others' lives suddenly found surprising opportunities with the most unexpected people: doctors. It turned out they were always the ones asking me the same question:

"Doug, how did you get this job?"

It was an obvious question. I didn't fit the profile of most of their sales reps. I wasn't a good-looking, twenty-seven-year-old cheerleader standing there smiling at them. Instead I was a fifty-year-old man who always responded to their questions by saying, "Doctor, you don't want to know."

By this point in my life, I knew certain truths. One was that people loved desserts. So whenever I visited doctors' offices, I often walked in carrying a box of

Dairy Queen Dilly bars. Of course, I'd eat mine before I got there. If you could get a doctor to put a Dilly bar in his or her hand, that meant you had at least five minutes with them. I always taped my business card to the box as well, so whenever they would grab one from the freezer, they might wonder who brought them in and then see Doug Biegel's name on the card.

The Dilly bars gave me just enough time to make a connection with these doctors. Most of the ones I spoke to inevitably asked me the same question:

"How did you get this position?"

This was God saying to me, *It's your time to share about Me, Doug.* When I told them they didn't want to know, they always continued to ask, and after the third time they asked, I would answer in the same way.

"It's God's amazing grace and my big mouth that got me this job."

This allowed me to openly share my testimony and to be a witness for Jesus Christ. I realized you don't have to carry a Bible or beat someone over the head in order to share how God has impacted your life.

CHAPTER FIFTEEN

Say It Now

Don't wait to express your heart to the people in your life. You never know when they will be gone.

The last time I saw my father was at a nursing home on July 8, 2004. When I walked into the lobby and saw my parents, Dad smiled and said to Mom, "Here comes my son." We had a beautiful time together that day.

Every time I left my father, I always bid him goodbye with the following conversation:

"Dad, I have good news and bad news."

"What's the good news?" he asked.

"God is building you a mansion on the crystal sea, and He may put a little bakery on the back."

"So what's the bad news?"

"You're still here," I said.

"That ain't so bad."

The last time I spoke with him, I jokingly asked him for money.

"Dad, I need a hundred dollars."

With a poker-straight face, Dad replied, "Your mother has all the money."

"But if you had a hundred dollars, could I have it?"

"Absolutely."

"If I got it in twenties, how many would I get?"

Dad stared up at the ceiling for a moment, his mind thinking. "Five."

"And if I got it in tens, how many would I get?"

Once again, he looked up at the ceiling. "Ten."

"Dad, you're fine," I told him.

I kissed him goodbye and left. The next day, Dad got sick, and the following day he died.

I cried more thinking about my dad's funeral than while I was at his funeral. This is because when he died, we had said everything we needed to say.

He knew I'm the man I am today because of him and my mom.

He knew I could see their commitment to their family, their work, and most importantly, to the Lord.

My father's generosity was second to none when it came to giving to the school and the church. He gave his time, his talents, and his money, and that's where I learned to give my due.

I'm the man I am today because of my father and my mother. I remind my mother of this all the time, just like I used to tell my father.

Sometimes it's not always easy to simply share how much you love and appreciate someone else. But do it today. Don't assume there will be a tomorrow when you can finally speak your mind.

CHAPTER SIXTEEN

From Baking to Steel

"Okay, God . . . where are You? What am I supposed to do?"

I had been at this place in my life before. First in 1978 when the family bakery burned to the ground. Then in 1985 when Marilyn died. Now it was 2010 and the job I had grown to love over the last eight years was gone.

THE BAKER'S SON

I was fifty-seven years old with Jana and Paul still at home, a mortgage, and no job. Once again, God's amazing grace got me through this tough time.

Early in 2010, the pharmaceutical industry went through major changes as certain patents were expiring and new patents were not being approved. This meant downsizing was going to happen. In June of that year, every salesperson was told they had to stay home to wait for a call from their manager. Mine came at 8:40 one morning. I knew the moment the phone rang that I was going to be among the first to be let go.

"I'm sorry, Doug. You didn't make the cut. Do not go out anymore and promote medications."

Once again my world was shattered. But God always picks up the pieces.

For several months I was unemployed and floundering around, feeling desperate and borderline depressed. The whispers kept ringing in my ears. *You're fifty-seven. Nobody wants to hire a fifty-seven-year-old.* People knew I made a lot of money in my former job. They also were afraid that if they gave me a job, I might be gone in six months. So I didn't get any offers for three months.

In the fall of 2010, I received a call from a local industrial manufacturing company and ended up working for them as a commissioned salesman. This means if I don't sell, we don't eat. Once again God showed me His faithfulness. I stopped at any place with a smokestack to see if I could drum up some business. My first sale was to a brewery in Munster, Indiana. I was the only person in the building that did not have a tattoo or body piercing. They have since become good friends and I still do business with them to this day.

This steel fabrication company specialized in making structural steel, such as mezzanines, staircases, handrails, safety gates, and caged ladders on the outside of buildings. Did I know all the tools or how all of those things were made? No. But one of my gifts is the ability to maintain and keep good relationships. As I always say, people don't care what you know until they know that you care. When you care about people and show you are interested in them, you will get your fair share of orders, whatever the product might be.

I would go into someone's office and see photos, so I'd ask about their children. If I saw a picture of them with a fish, I'd ask them about their hobby. Whenever I saw a bunch of sports memorabilia, I engaged them in a discussion about athletics. There are a few things you can ask people about without offending them, such as their hobbies, what they do in their spare time, and their family. Most of the time that will break the ice enough to ask for an order.

In my role at this new company, I didn't need to know everything about steel fabrication. I still don't. I'm the middleman. I find people who need work done; then I find people to do it, and I connect them and I add a markup for my time. I give the customer whatever they want, whatever their needs happen to be.

As salesmen do, they ask other salesmen for leads to new customers. One day I was told to go and see an engineer at a large candy company, so I walked in carrying two strudels. He just so happened to be a wannabe baker. In one hour I got up enough courage to ask for the order. I have had men working there since 2011. For a commissioned salesman, that is a great steady paycheck. God has blessed me and Debbie so much with this customer, and in doing so, we have been able to help many others.

All glory, honor, and praise be given to Him.

When it comes to stewardship and generosity related to finances, there are two Dougisms I use all the time:

1. "Pay God, pay yourself, then pay your bills. In that order. You'll never have a problem if you do it in that order."
2. "Love people and use things. Keep in this order. If you love things and use people, you have a problem."

Generosity starts with having an attitude of gratitude, with showing a readiness to give more of something like time or money than is necessary or expected.

The ingredients to be someone who gives don't simply consist of money. You can give many things to others: your time, your talents, your love. I'm pretty strict about giving generously. In order to do so, I not only have the necessary ingredients, but I also have the proven recipes. My parents didn't just show me how to bake cakes and banket and other treats. They let me know what giving to others looked like.

Generosity doesn't have to come in the form of a check or cash. Anybody can show generosity. It can be seen in cutting someone's lawn or shoveling a neighbor's snow. In calling someone who is sick or buying groceries for somebody. In helping a friend who is lonely or helping someone with homework. As I said, generosity starts with an attitude of gratitude.

I've never stopped baking since the bakery burned down. This baking is too much for a hobby, not enough for a living, and I'm too stupid to quit. To this day I still do it and still love it.

For me, I enjoy selling my baked goods at craft shows and fundraisers. What God has shown me is that baking is another way I can share my testimony and generosity.

One day I was talking to a clerk at a store where I sell my strudel. Her son had committed suicide six months earlier. I was able to share a little of my own story with her. Soon we were both bawling in the aisle of the store. I would have loved to have this book so I could give it to her and say, "Take this book home and read it, and if you have any questions, call me."

I want to give anybody that opportunity. We all have a story, and we all have questions. The most important gift I can give anybody at this point in my life is time. None of us can get time back. We can't duplicate or reproduce time, so the way I spend it is really important to me. I'm not big into nonsense things, and I don't want to waste time. What I want is to make a significant difference in people's lives. If one of those people can be you, please let me have this opportunity!

CHAPTER SEVENTEEN

Making an Impact

On Sunday morning, December 17, 2017, I sat in the church pew while everybody around me stood and sang. Something was not quite right.

"Dad, what is wrong?" Mark asked me after coming over to see me.

Debbie already knew something was wrong since she had thought my driving wasn't so good on the ride to church.

The next thing I remember, I'm being wheeled out

of the church sanctuary by Mark and his friend. Our pastor stopped the service and prayed, then fifty feet later he realized it was me, so he prayed again for me by name. I do not recommend passing out in church, but if you absolutely have to, Faith Church in Highland, Indiana, is a great place to do it. There were so many people in the narthex waiting to help me.

Mark knew I felt anxious, so he got down on all fours in order for us to be eye to eye.

"Dad, let's repeat some Scripture," Mark said.

He didn't know my condition; he just knew I was scared. There are no words to say how happy I felt when I heard him wanting to recite Scripture. Praise God! I had just finished teaching Zeke, my grandson, how to memorize John 3:16 two words at a time. "For God." "So loved." "The world." "That He." "Gave His." "Only Son." I didn't feel anxious as I recited God's promise to me while lying in the back of the church:

> "For I know the plans I have," declares the
> Lord, "plans to give you a hope and a future, to
> help you and not harm you."

I did get a little upset when all five of my children, including my two daughters from Michigan, along with many of the spouses showed up at my bedside. A few days in the hospital and many tests determined I'd had a stroke and my heart was occasionally in A-fib. After new meds, rest, and several trips to the cardiologist, I am doing much better. Once again God has shown me His faithfulness.

The health scare at the end of 2017 was a reminder to me of my story and testimony summed up in one sentence.

God is faithful in times of joy and sorrow.

Anytime the question of mortality comes along in life, it allows you to pause and remember all those you love and who love you. To think about those who have made the biggest impact on your life.

As Mark lay beside me on the floor of the church to provide comfort to his father, I could still picture the four-year-old boy sleeping on the church stairs in the middle of his father's wedding. I also remembered his wedding almost two decades later when I was his best man.

THE BAKER'S SON

On August 5, 2006, our son Mark married Marissa. It was a special day. He gave Debbie a special gift on this occasion. After Marilyn passed away, I gave some of the diamonds from her wedding ring to each of my children. Mark had his diamond made into a pendant and gave it to Debbie. He also put some of the diamonds in his wife's wedding band. Mark has a big heart, and there's always a certain calmness I feel whenever he enters the room. He and I don't even have to talk to communicate; we just look at each other and know what we're thinking.

My children are amazing. They're all really, really special people. Each of them carries special parts of me, just like I carry special memories of each of them. There are too many to write down. They have all impacted me in different ways, helping to shape the person I am today.

Pamela Ann, my oldest child, is a chip off the old block. She is just like her father, someone who wants to know when something is going to start, how long it's going to last, and when it will be over. She is outgoing, aggressive, and has a huge love for those whose voice is not often heard. Pam will not back down to get what those not often heard need. She will be their advocate and always do what is right for them. Pam loves the Lord and her family. I am proud to see her leading Reflectors, a special-needs ministry at the church.

Amy is most like Marilyn. Her "happy place" is being with her family, enjoying some activity with her boys. She has a big heart for children, impacting, teaching, and just loving them. She loves when her nieces, Ashlee or Nina, can sit by her. Amy loves the Lord and her family. Often when she walks into a room, her first words are "What can I do?" She is always ready to help.

Jana Lee has been a joy to be around since the day she was born. She works hard at whatever she does. She is a born leader and always willing to help others. While in junior high, Jana helped me study for my pharmaceutical testing. Each night she would quiz me to see what I learned that day. Jana loves the Lord and her husband, Brent. She is so supportive of Brent and his work as a youth leader at their church. When Jana is around, she is always helping wherever she can.

Paul Joseph completed Team Biegel. He is a gifted leader in everything he does. More than once the ladies in the office of his high school have said, "Paul runs this school." He has a strong independent mind and always thinks before he says anything. Paul loves the Lord and

Kayla. They work well together, especially when they are working at Kayla's family farm. Paul is always willing to help, whatever the task.

Impacting others and helping is in the DNA of all the Biegel children. As their father, I am deeply grateful for that. My "happy place" is being together with the entire family. When we're together, if anybody asks me what I need, I always give them the same answer:

"I need nothing."

Everything I need is surrounding me.

One day I received a surprise call from someone who used to go to our church.

"Doug—I'm in Ely, Minnesota, standing in front of the outfitters we used in 1976. You impacted my life forty-four years ago. Thank you!"

I was twenty-three years old at the time when four of us men in church took eight boys to Canada for a week. I can't believe their parents let us go. I've remained in touch with some of this group.

"You can't impact people unless you're willing to pour into their life and mentor them one on one. And you mentored us boys forty-four years ago. Because of that impact, I'm able to share Jesus Christ. We have to do a trip like that again sometime."

"I'll do it again if we all bring one person along to impact," I told him. "I don't want to go just to do it."

That call made me think of Harry Heersema, the first man other than my dad who left footprints in the sand that pointed me to Jesus Christ. He was the leader for our boys' group in church. At the time, he was single. Later on in life, he married a woman who lost her husband and had four children. Harry was a man of God who poured his life into us boys. Like our group of four did later in life, Harry took a large group of us boys up to Canada on a trip. Recently Harry passed away and went to his heavenly home. I'm friends with his children and occasionally talk to them.

Another man who made an impact on me when I was young was our pastor, Reverend Bill Brownson. He had four boys and the family lived in the parsonage next to the church, several blocks away from our bakery. Many days Reverend Brownson came home on his lunch break wearing his white long-sleeved shirt and tie. Since I was friends with his sons, we'd be in his backyard playing baseball. Reverend Brownson would pitch since we didn't have a pitcher. I can't tell you how

THE BAKER'S SON

many windows we broke in the parsonage because the lot was too small! Today I remain in contact with Dr. Bill Brownson by phone. He is an elderly, godly man who is still impacting my life.

These two men, along with many others, helped to shape me into the man I would become. My goal in life has been to make an impact for Christ ever since developing my holy boldness. I still remember one doctor I had gotten to know while I worked in pharma sales. His secretary's son passed away, so I went to the wake and visited with the family. The doctor was amazed that I would take personal time to come to something like this. I shared with him that my aunt spent thirty-five years working as a missionary in India; then I basically shared my life story of how God has walked with me through good times and bad.

The next time I saw the doctor, my boss was with me. The doctor bragged about me in front of him. I thanked him for the compliments when I saw him again.

"Doug, those weren't just nice things I said," the doctor told me. "That's how I feel. You're welcome here anytime."

As a new pharmaceutical rep, a man named Herschel

had a huge impact on my life and career. We worked our territory together for over six years. As an African American, Herschel taught me not to see color. We were the same height and weight, so we would tell everybody we were twins. I still touch base with him every so often.

I keep in touch with a lot of people. The fact is I'm a people person, and I have a lot of time in the car riding from one account to another. It's not unusual for me to pick up the phone and spend five minutes talking to someone when they come to mind.

Paul and Hank are two people I call every now and then. They were both my immediate supervisors at different times at the manufacturing company, and both men made an impact on me.

One of the things I do well is to network. I never burn a bridge; I always leave on good terms with others. For sales, you just never know when you're going to have to use that source again. You also never know just how you might be able to help encourage or impact someone else on any given day.

I've come to learn that a lot of people are reluctant to share the truth of what is going on in their lives, both the good and the bad. They think it's better to be middle-of-the-road with their conversations. Some people are afraid to share their story, their *real* story. That doesn't make it right or wrong; that's who we are. The challenge in life for Christians is to make them realize they have a story that's impactful for the Kingdom. And they can't keep that story to themselves.

If I didn't tell people about my banket, I would be making it at home for Debbie and myself. It's the same thing with sharing your faith. It's not really an option but a command, yet we're so reluctant to do it. Will we lose our salvation if we don't share it with others? No. Will there be a few more people in line for heaven because we shared?

I sure hope so.

You need to walk a mile in someone else's shoes before you can share Jesus Christ. My way to do this was always telling my story like I'm doing now.

Many times I've heard the same sort of comment:

"Doug, I just don't have the boldness you do. How can I make an impact on anybody?"

I always reply that one of the easiest ways to do this is to ask someone how you can pray for them. As I always say, people don't care what you know until they know that you care. If you care about someone, you've got a foot in the door. So when you tell someone you want to pray for them, you're invited in. That will lead to some other thing. Maybe not that day, maybe at some other time. Commit to pray for somebody else by writing it down and then following through. God will take care of the rest.

CHAPTER EIGHTEEN

Walking Alongside Others

Sometimes we have to slow down in order to hear what God is trying to tell us.

A few years ago, Debbie and I took a cruise. One day, we had gone ashore for an excursion, and I started to not feel well. Debbie wanted to go sightseeing to look at some rock formations or something like that, so I told her to go on without me.

"Debbie, just go get me a Coke. I'll stay in the bus."

I spent the next hour with God, praying and asking for His help.

God, please don't let me get sick here in the middle of nowhere. Thank You for everything You've done in my life.

God answered my prayers. Debbie came back from her excursion and I ended up being fine. Those moments in that bus were a warning that none of us are promised tomorrow. Nobody knows how much time we have left in this world. They were also a reminder of the blessings God has given me.

Now more than ever I wanted to put my story down on paper. I didn't want to just tell the elevator pitch. I wanted to share a few more details, especially with those I love the most.

What I didn't know was how writing this book would allow me to grieve the significant losses in my life. It turned out I had never really slowed down enough in my life to do that.

There is no recipe for grief. No instructions for how long it will take to get through your loss. I didn't do a very good job after Marilyn passed away. It was hard to grieve when you came home exhausted from work and had three kids looking at you and asking what was for dinner. All I know is that you can't know what it's like until you've been there.

I've been there, so I do know. And this is the advice I can give anybody who has lost someone dear in their life.

Take one day at a time.

Look to Jesus for your strength.

In all of life, you need to crawl before you walk, and you need to walk before you run.

Grief is a process. It's a journey, not a destination.

Just remember: this moment doesn't define your life. It's something you're going through, something painful and difficult, and there's no getting around that fact.

It's normal to be angry at God. But remember that God is good. Recognize that being angry isn't good for you, but God is good.

Not long ago, a man I knew at Gun Lake dealt with the loss of his wife. She had battled cancer for years and he had been caring for her throughout. When I saw her at church, I always greeted her and told her I was glad to see her. I didn't tell her she looked great because she didn't. I told her the truth that it was a blessing to see her.

After this woman died, I kept in touch with her husband by calling him. I would call to check in with him, to be honest about what I knew he was going through.

"I just want you to know, Easter is going to be rough," I said. "I want to make sure you get your butt out of bed. I want to make sure you put one foot in front of the other. And I want you to know I love you."

To this day I will occasionally call him once or twice a month. Sometimes I talk to him, and if I don't reach him, I leave a message. He returns my calls to thank me for remembering him and always tells me I'm amazing.

"I'm not amazing. I've walked the street that you're walking, and I know how much it hurts. I know how nice it is to have somebody to talk to you instead of looking at you like you got leprosy."

Losing Marilyn taught me a big lesson in life. Happiness is a choice. As I always say, you attract more bees with honey than vinegar. And if you've chosen to be the honey rather than the vinegar, you'll attract more people.

Happiness is a choice for all of us, and it's certainly a difficult choice to make when you've lost a loved one.

There was a young father I got to know who was wrestling with his child becoming gravely sick. He reached a point where he was upset with God and everybody else around him. I took him out to dinner to try to encourage him and to pull him aside and slap him around a bit.

"You can be mad at me, but you can't be mad at God," I told him.

I gave him a copy of *Jesus Calling* by Sarah Young.

"Read one of these devotions every day," I said. "I'm going to be here with you. We're going to get through this. I don't know what the outcome will be, but I'll walk beside you and I'll be there for you. This is something you'll work out. But your attitude is a big part of it."

Thankfully their child became well again and is a normal kid able to live his life. This young man and his wife have devoted their lives to impacting kids who are sick. They are in a place they wouldn't have chosen, but they're trying to impact families who are going through the same thing. Recently I saw their child playing basketball, so I sent the father a text.

I'm so glad you're willing to share your story. So proud to be your friend. I still remember a time when we went out to dinner and things weren't so good.

God has given me opportunities to make an impact

with others through my own pain and grief. I have a friend who lost his wife, so we have taken men out for breakfast who are going through the same thing. We don't give him some set of rules and ways to deal with his grief. We simply talk to him and share our stories. We will recommend things to do, such as getting a housekeeper so that someone can come in and do your laundry, buy groceries, and keep your house clean.

"I understand your wife passed away," I told a man recently. "My wife died many years ago . . ."

I start to share my story to let him know that I understand, that I've been there. The best thing anybody can do for someone who is grieving the loss of a spouse, a child, or a parent is to walk beside them.

We all have moments where we feel desperate, full of questions and ready to jump off the wall. You don't have to lose a loved one to experience anxiety about the world.

One day a man in his mid-forties opened up about his fears and concerns. He didn't know what he was doing or where he was going in life. Everything seemed to be going wrong with him.

"I have three things to tell you," I told him. "Get a pen and write this down."

First off, I shared Philippians 4:4-6 with this man. "Rejoice in the Lord always. I will say it again: Rejoice! Let your gentleness be evident to all. The Lord is near. Do not be anxious about anything, but in every situation, by prayer and petition, with thanksgiving, present your requests to God." I told him he had a week to memorize that and come back to quote it to me.

Next, I said he needed to get a three-by-five card, then write Jeremiah 29:11 on it. "'For I know the plans I have for you,' declares the Lord, 'plans to prosper you and not to harm you, plans to give you hope and a future.'"

"Put that on your mirror in your bathroom," I suggested. "I want you to read it out loud every morning." The third bit of advice I gave him was to call my financial adviser and make an appointment with him. After that first meeting with the financial guy, the man called me up to thank me. He told me he realized that he and his wife needed to change their lifestyle.

We can all make an impact on people in our lives. This man called me up simply to bellyache, but I turned it into an opportunity to encourage him and be an example for Christ.

EPILOGUE

I sit in a familiar spot by the shore, staring out at a lake full of life and activity. It's Labor Day weekend, and I'm finishing my fifty-fourth summer at Shady Shores. Gun Lake is my happy place, where I come to rest and relax. I'm grateful that it's only 140 miles away; carving out two hours to drive to this haven is worth it.

As a teenager we worked hard each week so we could head to Gun Lake as a family. Saturdays were especially busy at the bakery so that we could leave early afternoon to enjoy a few hours of sunlight on the water. My parents brought bakery goods for the neighbors to enjoy while I headed to the lake to water-ski. Sundays were family days that included church in the morning and at night. We were allowed to swim on Sunday afternoons, which was very relaxing.

Since June of 1967, Gun Lake has been an oasis for our entire family. In 1980 I purchased my first place at Gun Lake. When Marilyn and I were raising Pam, Amy, and Mark, weekends at Gun Lake were a highlight for us. Some of the children took their first steps at Gun Lake. As the family grew, we were able to enjoy Gun Lake along with sports, friends, and all the busyness of a young family.

In 1986, while dating Debbie, she would often go with the children and me to see what the attraction to Gun Lake was. In 1988 we were able to purchase a trailer in the lot we are currently in, and a year later we purchased a double-wide trailer for this lot we are still using. As the children continued to grow, the lake was always a priority and most weekends all of us would come here. We left after work on Friday as soon as it was possible to get all seven of us in the van, returning home Sunday night after church.

EPILOGUE

As the children were married and out of the house, we slowly began to be able to leave earlier on Fridays. For a long time, our goal was to be at the lake by dinnertime to join our neighbors for dinner. The last few years we try to leave Thursday after work, which makes for a longer weekend. Currently we try to be at the lake by suppertime on Thursdays.

Today my mother and sister Janice live in the place that my mom and dad bought. It is forty-five feet from the lake with a beautiful view. We gather, as a family, for a cup of coffee, to visit my mom or just to relax and be together. It is a safe and comfortable place.

Shady Shores has been a strong community and a great place to raise a family. We're thankful for the closeness here, for all the friends we've known, especially all those on Fir Lane. We all come from different places, different churches, and there is a big variety of ages, but what brings us together is the Lord. We have stood together in times of happiness and sadness. I can think of many weddings and funerals I've been to with families around here. When these friends have had their backs against the wall, I hope I'm the first person to pick up the phone to let them know I'm thinking about them. I know we have to enjoy the moment with everyone who's here, because things in life always change. Some are older and not as healthy as they used to be.

For a moment, I think about the plans I have for this weekend. Just like every Labor Day holiday, we're planning to take all the water toys out of the water and put them in storage. All the docks will be taken out of the water, and we will remove all the flowers. There is cleaning to do and things to set in order. That's the plan.

Plans. We all have them. Our to-do lists, our tasks that need to be done, our schedules, and our appointments.

You never know when God has a different plan. When your plans will suddenly be thrown out the window. When life as you know it will suddenly and drastically change.

I had lots of plans when we closed down the trailer on Labor Day, September 2, 1985. Marilyn and I left the lake with eight-year-old Pam, five-year-old Amy, and two-year-old Mark. It was like any other time for our family of five. None of us knew that ten days later, Marilyn would pass away.

This time of year always reminds me of that last Labor Day weekend with Marilyn. When I think of her,

EPILOGUE

I don't want her back for a minute. I know she's walking streets of gold. But I hope God opens heaven's window so she can see these kids and grandkids and how well they turned out. I hope she can see their smiles and hear their laughter. I hope she can watch them on the water and picture them playing. I hope she knows what incredible people they are.

I'm amazed that even though Marilyn has been gone for thirty-five years, I'm still talking about her. How can you have feelings for someone who's been gone for that long? My father's been gone sixteen years. I still miss him.

For I know the plans I have for you, Doug. Plans to prosper you and not to harm you, plans to give you hope and a future.

God had plans that Labor Day weekend back in 1985. God has plans for me on this Labor Day weekend, too.

When I close my eyes and picture my mom, I see a very content lady reading her Bible or praying while enjoying the view of the lake. To this day she still has a huge impact on my life. My mother is a very godly woman.

She keeps a journal with people's names written in it, and she prays for them by name along with Debbie and the children and grandchildren every day.

Since my mom thinks I do not work, she will call me whenever she has a thought to discuss with me. I talk to my mom more than I see her. When my back is against the wall, whether it's business-related or trying to impact someone for Jesus or a health issue, I can go to my mother and know that if I ask her to pray about something, she will. I also know we can celebrate the victories when God answers a prayer and we often do.

My mother turned ninety on October 19, 2020. She is very outspoken about loving the Lord, and she's very concerned about those not walking with the Lord, with people on the outskirts of faith. She just loves people, plain and simple.

I love my mom. Since I was a child, my mother always believed in me and still tells me that often. Mom reminds me that God has been faithful to me.

Mom still misses my father. We frequently talk about Dad when we are together as a family. A while ago when I was taking an oven apart with Mark, I told him how proud Grandpa would be to see him working on it. We discussed how my father would have had the ability to do many things if he had only had the proper tools. He was old-school—he'd buy a bigger hammer and a bigger drill.

One thing my father and I shared in common remains to this day: we couldn't talk about our family and faith without being reduced to tears. Dad's excuse was "I'm sorry. I'm on a lot of medication." I simply say, "I'm sorry—I'm a Biegel. I come by it naturally." When I share my faith or talk about my family, my eyes can't help but start to well up because of the love and devotion I have for both.

"If baking is any labor at all, it's a labor of love. A love that gets passed from generation to generation." An author named Regina Brett said that, and I believe it's true. It's been sixteen years since my father passed away. I know he wouldn't be surprised a bit to find me still baking. We were born to be bakers and have done it the best we could.

My plan is to stop baking on December 31, 2022. That's the plan, the end date. I will be sixty-nine years old and Debbie will be sixty-three. That seems like a reasonable goal.

Baking has always been mindless work for me, and I like it. I'm making a good product and helping people earn some money. It's a bit of a head rush having all these people asking, "How do you do this?" and saying, "This is amazing." It's encouraging to go to craft shows and to hear compliments about my treats. I love hearing the stories, but I am always thinking, *Maybe next year I'll stop.*

When people ask me about retiring, I say in order to retire, you have to have a job. I feel I don't have one. If you enjoy what you do, you'll never work a day in your life. And that's where I'm at now. I thank God for the people I'm affiliated with now. They've given me a lot of freedom to do the things I love.

Baking has been more of a seasonal thing, starting from the first of June and going to the end of December. I'm so grateful that Debbie lets me do this in our house, especially since it can be messy. She is part of the business, decorating all of the cakes.

I thought my childhood was fairly normal even though we lived above the bakery. It wasn't until many years later that I realized the impact that bakery has had on my life. That's one of the many things writing this book has taught me. The light finally went on.

EPILOGUE

Doug, you've never been away from food. Never.

I grew up a baker's son and grew to have the same aspirations. When the bakery burned down, the plans for making cakes continued. I met Marilyn through delivering bread to the Holland Home. After she passed away and I started to talk with Debbie, part of my initial flirting with her was when I taught her how to write on and decorate cakes. I told her how good she was at it; I wasn't lying.

Today I don't ever show up anywhere without some sort of food. My little thing these days is to bring shrimp at Christmas.

"Uncle Doug, are you going to bring shrimp?"

"You bet I am."

And when Debbie and I go anywhere or are invited, we bring something nice. I don't bring a bag of chips. Somebody else can do this. If that's okay for you, that's fine. I tend to think a little bigger and I'm blessed to be able to.

Maida Heatter, a cookbook author dubbed "the Queen of Desserts" who passed away at 102 years of age, said this about baking: "Happiness is baking cookies. Happiness is giving them away. And serving them, and eating them, talking about them, reading and writing about them, thinking about them, and sharing them with you."

I agree with Maida. Happiness is also my family. Serving my family and eating with them and talking with them. And happiness is definitely my faith. Talking and writing and sharing my faith with others.

Baking and food have been a way to share my faith with others. Everybody loves dessert. It brings people together. Especially Biegels' banket.

I hear Debbie calling my name down Fir Lane. I look and picture the young lady I brought here on Memorial Day weekend in 1986, the girl I didn't get a chance to fully get to know before I married her. We went on dates and I saw a lot of her, but I also had three young kids. I always kept things real and wanted her to know that we were going to do stuff alone one day. Now fast-forward all these years, we're empty nesters and Debbie is the one that I would rather spend time with more than anybody else. Our rides to and from Michigan are holy ground for us. I just don't want to be without her. When she talks about going to Florida to see her folks, I'm encouraging her to do that. But the truth is

EPILOGUE

I don't want to be alone. I need Debbie and my family. I need people.

It's amazing to think how this woman I love and treasure has been by my side in good times and bad times for thirty-three years. Debbie has believed in me and always encouraged me to do my best. What a blessing.

God did have a plan. A beautiful one.

Trust Me from the bottom of your heart, Doug. Don't try to figure out everything on your own. Listen for My voice in everything you do, everywhere you go; I am the one who will keep you on track.

What a faithful God.

God's faithfulness is not over in my life, and neither are His blessings or the trials He will see me through. As long as He gives me strength, I will praise His name and share Him with others. I do not know what the future holds, but I know who holds the future and I know He holds my hand.

Hi, my name is Doug Biegel. I make handmade pastries from my family's one-hundred-year-old recipes. All Biegel's Cakery products are made without any preservatives. Our main pastries are banket, cookies, and fruit-filled strudel.

My story? In ten months' time, I bought a home, had a child, had major surgery, and then witnessed a fire to my family business that wiped out everything. Seven and a half years later, I woke up and my wife Marilyn was dead in bed. But you know what? God was faithful.

God is faithful in good times and bad.

So I've shared my story. What is *your* story and who have you shared it with? That's what the great commission tells us to do. To share it with others.

You can start by sharing it with me.

ACKNOWLEDGMENTS

This book has been percolating in my mind for a long time. I did not know how to get it out of my mind and onto paper. Travis Thrasher has been a conduit able to articulate my thoughts, feelings, and emotions. Thank you, Travis, for all of your hard work.

Team Biegel has been a source of blessings to me for many years. Without Debbie, Pam, Amy, Mark, Jana, and Paul, this journey would have been more difficult. Dan, Al, Marissa, Brent, and Kayla—each of you have joined my journey at different times. Some of these stories you may have heard many times; others may be new to you or maybe you have not even heard them. I am so glad you're a part of our family. I love that you love Jesus and my children.

Together we are a stronger, tighter team. We have held each other together through difficult times and happy times. God has been faithful to us through each and every opportunity and challenge.

THE BAKER'S SON

Ethan, Trevor, Isaac, Tyler, Ashlee, Drew, Zeke, Nina, Mollee, and Megan: Papa loves you so much! Always remember whose you are: You are God's children and Papa Biegel's grandchildren!

Yes, that is twenty-two. God has been so faithful with our beautiful family. Praise Him! Also, our faithful God has held our hands through difficult times. Three of my children have had multiple miscarriages. I do not know that pain personally but after walking through that with them, I know God held our hands. He is always faithful even when we go through difficult times.

Marissa said, "There are many Biegel cousins in heaven and I know they are being cared for." What I think she meant to say is, "There are many Biegel cousins in heaven and Marilyn will be taking care of them." Marissa, I promise that Marilyn is walking streets of gold with those cousins and she and Grandpa Joe are taking good care of each one.

There is a plaque in our kitchen that says, "We may not have it all together but . . . together we have it all." That pretty well sums up Team Biegel.

I have been blessed with many solid relationships. Some old, some new, some older, some young. I have many people I can call to get advice and encouragement.

ACKNOWLEDGMENTS

You know who you are. My journey would not have been as rich as it is without you, but because of you I am a better man.

This book is dedicated to my Lord Jesus Christ. He gets all honor, glory, and praise. This is my story about the baker's son. As I said, be thinking of your story and always be prepared to share it with somebody else.

My story is not finished, and neither is God's faithfulness. I cannot wait to see how God will use my story and me. I desire to finish strong, point others to Him, and give Him the glory. If you want to know Him better, please do not be afraid to reach out to me.

Don't worry about the bus; I'll bring you home.

PS: On February 18, 2021, Mollee Joy Lamberts and Megan Sue Lamberts were born, approximately 11 weeks early. Both girls are doing well and are growing each day. If all goes as planned, Lord willing and with answered prayers, the girls will be home in May or June 2021. God has blessed our family with two new granddaughters. Praise His holy name! Now Team Biegel totals twenty-two and counting. I cannot wait to see what other blessings God has for our family.